"LOS BILITOS":

the
story
of

"BILLY THE KID"

AND HIS GANG

Charles Frederick Rudulph
1854—1914

A member of sheriff Pat Garrett's posse when they captured Billy the Kid and his gang at El ojo Del Taiba on December 24, 1880.
Wife: Emilia Pendaries
Children: John, Margaret, Louis, Dick, Marie.

"LOS BILITOS":

the
story
of

"BILLY THE KID"

AND HIS GANG

As told by Charles Frederick Rudulph
- a member of Garrett's
historical posse.

An aged manuscript
handwritten in 1880
- discovered in 1976.

by LOUIS LEON BRANCH

A Hearthstone Book

Carlton Press, Inc.   New York, N.Y.

Dedicated to
Charles Frederick Rudulph,
"One of the many, unsung heroes of the West,"
and to
his father, Milnor,
"A friend of the Kid's."

Acknowledgements

Mil Gracias to Mrs. Martina Sanchez of Mora for the use of her valuable papers; the memory of Mr. Tom McGarth of Las Vegas and his heirs for granting me permission to use their copyrighted photograph of Billy the Kid and Pat Garrett, and for allowing me to photograph and reproduce the old Las Vegas City jail door and handcuffs, as well as for an exciting tour of his home museum; to Mr. Dennis Branch of Santa Fe for his pragmatically illustrative sketches and photos; to the whole Rudulph (Rudolph) family of New Mexico for the use of their historic name; to all previous researchers and historians, amateur or professional, for their contribution in bringing to light an exciting and eventful period of New Mexican history.

To Walter Noble Burns, author of *The Saga of Billy the Kid;* William A. Keleher, who wrote *Violence In Lincoln County;* Frazier Hunt, author of *The Tragic Days of Billy The Kid;* and Pat F. Garrett, who wrote *The Authentic Life of Billy The Kid.*

To: the New Mexico State Archives, and the New Mexico State Library for such splendid and valuable reference material; to *The Santa Fe New Mexican,* and *The Las Vegas Daily Optic* for their immense contributions; and to my family for their patience and assistance.

Contents

Introduction

This book is a compilation of proven facts, unsubstantiated stories (some told by the Kid himself), but most importantly, it is a completely new addition to the annals of the Billy the Kid adventure, a firsthand eyewitness account written between 1880 and 1881 by Charles F. Rudulph, a member of Sheriff Pat Garrett's posse, on the subject of the search for, the capture at El Ojo Del Taiba, and the subsequent death of Billy the Kid.

The yellowed manuscript, discovered in a northern New Mexico mountain village in 1976, sheds some new light on an old topic a full one hundred years later.

The first section contains this author's own recounting of a well-known, oft written story, some of it history, some of it fallacy, but whether true or not, is what is universally known as the Billy the Kid story.

The second part contains the inclusion of the never-before-published story of the participation of the Rudulph clan in Billy's life, and this author's own translation and interpretation of Charles Rudulph's beautiful verses, written in fluent Spanish, on his stirring adventures.

There is no claim on my part of the authenticity of the entire story or lack of it or of the photographs of Pat Garrett and Billy the Kid as used for illustration, and owned by the estate of Tom McGrath of Las Vegas, New Mexico.

—Louis Leon Branch

Foreword

And so, the story of Billy the Kid continues. The saga, which had its birth about in 1872, still continues to unfold.

In 1976, two important discoveries were made: the Billy the Kid tombstone, which had been lost for decades, was found half-buried in a field in Texas, and the handwritten story, "La Campaña Sobre Los Bilitos," written between late 1880 and 1881 by Charles Frederick Rudulph, was unearthed in the beautiful, ancient village of Mora, almost a full century later. It carries us back in history to an era of the west long past but one which will never be forgotten. The outlaws and the gunmen, the heroes and the lawmen, were all a part of our continuously evolving history.

Billy the Kid was not a hero of his day; in fact, he could hardly be called a Robin Hood. He was an outlaw, a killer, and a thief, but it must be well remembered that so were the so-called lawmen who persecuted and pursued him. On their posses were hired killers, cattle rustlers and horse thieves, banded together with law abiding natives and ranchers.

Billy the Kid was known to have been a friendly, warmhearted young man, always the gentleman with womanhood, but also ruthless, daring and courageous with his enemies.

In those violent, unsettling days, it was either kill or be killed, and except for one unfortunate instance, Billy the Kid always slyly avoided the latter.

Since the character of Billy the Kid has received such very careful scrutiny and his biographers have gone from one extreme to the other (one even calls him a female impersonator), let us also examine the lives of the men who were his enemies, the evil seed that engendered the Lincoln County War.

I came across the aged, one-hundred year old manuscript written by my great uncle, on January 2, 1976. Even though its existence had been known within my family for almost a hundred years, I myself had never heard of it. The first one to mention it was my mother, Marie Trambley Branch, whose parents were Matilde Rudulph, (sister to my great uncle), and Frank Leon Trambley.

Knowing of my interests as an amateur historian, bottle dump archaeologist, and collector of anything old I can get my hands on, she told me one day: "There was a story written by my Uncle Charlie Rudulph in 1880 that you probably would be interested in. It was about Billy the Kid, and about when Uncle Charles was a member of the sheriff's posse that captured him."

For many years I had known that his father, Milnor Rudulph, had been president of the coroner's jury at the inquest at the Kid's death, but this was the first time that I had heard of Charles Rudulph's having been a member of Garrett's historical posse.

Even though my mother thought the old manuscript was in San Diego, by that afternoon, without even mentioning it again, I would be looking through the ancient pages.

While visiting an aunt whom I hadn't seen for a long time and rarely visited, she suddenly stood up and went to a bureau drawer, dug out a yellowed envelope, and handed it to me, saying: "It's a story about Billy the Kid written by my Tio Charley many years ago."

Whether it was the spirit of William Bonney or of Charles Rudulph I'll never know, but someone definitely wanted the old story brought to light, and had led me directly to it.

Perhaps it may have been the same spirit which led me that same afternoon to a cousin's house where, without having previously given it any thought, I received as a donation the old gristmill of my ancestors in Mora for its historical preservation and restoration.

The old rock mill had been scheduled for demolition that summer, but instead the St. Vrain-Trambley Mill Historical Foundation, dedicated to its preservation, was born that day. Thanks to the donor, Mr. Frank C. Trambley, the mill, built in 1864, will stand another hundred years.

Going back to the old manuscript, it is written in what appears to be a spiral type notebook of that era, bound with string instead of the metal binder of modern times. Its pages are yellowed with age, but completely legible, and everything considered, very well preserved. It is written in the beautiful script of those days and in the language of New Mexico in those days: Spanish.

Billy the Kid spoke fluent Spanish, as did Pat Garrett, Pete Maxwell, the Rudulphs, the Trambleys, the Branches, and all other frontiersmen who settled the west. They probably had to to survive, but soon they were an integral part of the Spanish, Indian and Mexican culture of the New Mexico Territory. Some of us would be absorbed into the culture, with only the foreign names remaining.

The first story, which is about the long search for and eventual capture of Billy the Kid and his gang, is written in verse and contains forty stanzas.

Its title is "La Campaña Sobre Los Bilitos," which translates, not too well, as: "Our Campaign Against Billy and His Gang." The title itself was surprising to me, since it was the first time that I had heard the gang referred to as "Los Bilitos." The location of the historical capture, "El Ojo Del Taiba," described by Charles Rudulph, is completely different from the "Stinking Springs" of all other writers of Billy the Kid lore. The exact location of the road leading to the springs, "El Camino del Tul," also mentioned in Rudulph's verses, has been lost in antiquity.

The second story, also in verse, is of Billy the Kid's escape and subsequent death at the hands of Sheriff Pat Garrett, and contains an additional sixteen stanzas. Its title is "Muerte Del Afamado Bilito," or, "Death of Famed Billy."

The old wine-colored notebook itself has about one hundred pages, complete with family poems, popular songs of the times, *Trobo de Chicoria y gracias*, *adevinanzas (riddles)*, etc. The Rudulph family of Sunnyside, Puerto de Luna and Rociada were obviously a well-educated, closely knit, loving family group.

Some of their affectionate poems written to one another in equally fluent Spanish or English, were on the diverse subjects of prolonged absences, occasions of happiness, the Billy the Kid story, devastating floods, the drought and epidemic of 1905, and the mere occasion of the opening of a new grist mill. The whole family wrote and recorded their poetry, some of which will be reprinted in this book.

Unknown and unsung by history, they were heroes of their times; their love and affection, so catching, lives on in the hearts of their descendants.

—The Author

Billy the Kid   *Pat Garrett*

BILLY THE KID WAS KILLED BY SHERIFF PAT
GARRETT ON JULY 15TH 1881 AT FORT SUMNER N.M.

P-46   Copyright Applied For by Tom McGarath   E.W. Post Card Co.
Albuquerque

Chapter One

Billy the Kid

On a cold day in November, 1869, his face hidden by the dust and grime of the frozen trail, there came to New Mexico a strange and enigmatic young man destined to build a legend unequalled in our time.

With his mother Catherine and his brother Joseph, he arrived in the territory, riding an old dusty covered wagon into the plaza of La Villa Real de la Santa Fe de San Francisco de Assisi. His name was William Henry McCarty, ten years old at the time. His strangeness, not evident until later, would lie in the fact that even after a hundred years, those who knew him and those who wrote and write of him still, cannot agree on who or what he was.

They called him Billy the Kid; some people called him just the Kid, or Kid Antrim, few of them knowing that his real name was William Henry Bonney and that he had also used the name Henry Antrim, his stepfather's name, and McCarty, his mother's maiden name.

The Spanish and Mexican peoples called him, *El Chivito*, meaning "kid goat," a term used synonymously with a rascal or a playful prankster, and he was also known affectionately as *El Bilito*, or "Little Billy."

Due to his vernal age, however, either name was fitting and descriptive. In English and Spanish, his famous diminutive Billy The Kid, fit him quite well.

In the last years of his life, Billy was also called, *El Chivato*, which means an old male goat, but then, only cynically by the opposing, warring faction who hated him with a passion, and would eventually cause his death.

Billy had abdicated their camp, and after giving it careful thought, joined forces with the other side. They were more representative of the people, he found, and as it turned out later, much closer to the law.

As we read through these pages, we should bear in mind the fact that even though Billy was almost always on the wrong side of the law, the group which persecuted him was also composed of unscrupulous outlaws and cutthroats, except that they wore a badge. Keeping up a false front of law and order, they harassed, ruined, and murdered their opposition, all in the name of the law.

On their posses were cattle rustlers and horse theives, highwaymen and vicious murderers, obviously hired for their noteworthy talent with a gun.

His persecutors were trying to salvage a powerful financial and political empire which was fast losing its grip. The tyrannical dynasty of the "Santa Fe Ring," whose immense powers had reached as far as Washington, D.C., was beginning to crumble.

When Billy's mother Catherine McCarty married William Henry Antrim in Santa Fe on March 1, 1873, with her were her two sons who signed as witnesses to the marriage and whose names were Henry McCarty, and Joseph McCarty. The couple were married in the Presbyterian Church by Reverend D.F. McFarland. Also witnessing the marriage were Mrs. A.R. McFarland and Miss Katie McFarland, probably the reverend's wife and daughter, and also Mr. Harvey Edwards. The groom according to this information was born in Anderson, Indiana on December 1, 1842, and was thirty years old.

It was Mr. Robert N. Mullin, formerly of Las Vegas, New Mexico, and later from El Paso, Texas, who unearthed the valuable piece of information. It is filed both in the records of the Santa Fe County archives and at the church parsonage archives in Santa Fe, and has officially laid to rest the claim that the couple had been married in Kansas, but also raises other questions in many a mind. Was it mere coincidence, that stepfather William Henry Antrim, and stepson William Henry McCarty had the same given name? And why, if Catherine McCarty resumed her maiden name when she moved to Colorado after her husband Bonney's death, did she give the name to her two sons?

Many unanswered questions, which of course, to her were private family matters and to us are history, went with her to the grave when she died soon after her marriage on September 16, 1874.

According to Ash Upson, historian, newsman and controversial ghost writer for Pat Garrett in his biography, *The Authentic Life Of Billy The Kid*, Billy was born in New York City on November 23, 1859.

Since the writing of Garrett's book was begun less than one year after Billy's death, we have to accept most of it as fact, even though the ghost writer's vivid imagination is a well-known fact. Many of his statements have been strongly disputed and discredited by later research.

According to Mr. Upson, Mrs. Antrim once told him that the family had moved to Coffeyville, Kansas in 1862, presumably from New York, and that Mr. Bonney, (no first name), Billy's father, had died there in 1864. After his death, she took her two boys to Colorado, and from there to Santa Fe in 1869, where they lived for about four years. She also mentioned that Billy was too young to remember his father, being only about five years old at the time of his death.

The family's three or four years in Santa Fe are not too well recorded except for the church records, but it is believed that Catherine operated a boardinghouse close to the old plaza.

Many old-timers claimed to have known Billy in those years, but their interviews were never properly recorded or verified. Their recollections, anyway, would be hard to believe, since at the time he was only between ten and thirteen years old. It is unreal for us to hope to glean from them any significant characteristics evident in the child and relate them to the character of the Kid as we knew him in later years.

17

Perhaps about all that can really be said is that those three or four years in Santa Fe may very well have been about the happiest years of Billy's life. He was an adventurous youth and probably had two or three *cuates* who chummed around with him.

The river, going right through town, always had plenty of cool, clear water and an abundance of fish. On a hot day in July, they could almost always be found at one of its many swimming holes, romping and wrestling on its green river banks. If they weren't there, they'd be at the *resbaladeros* or at the big pond at the bottom of Fort Marcy Road. They had a lot of fun skimming rocks on its clear surface or catching frogs. Mr. Vernier would give them a penny for every frog they would catch for him. Some people said he ate the legs, but who was going to believe that; he probably fed them to his cat.

Everyone who had any business in Santa Fe camped by the pond, tying their wood laden burros or sulkies to the trees around it as they went about their business in the dusty plaza.

Sometimes if the boys were lucky, they would see an old Indian chief in full regalia or one of the old fur trappers from Taos, like Ceran St. Vrain or Kit Carson or Alexander K. Branch. Some of them still wore nothing but buckskin shirts and leather breeches and hats, and Indian mocassins. They carried a knife in its scabbard always at the hip, and a beautiful 45-60 Winchester at their side. You just knew they had been brave Indian fighters, or had been out hunting buffalo.

If the men came to town without their wives or squaws, they'd make a beeline for one of the saloons which ringed the plaza. Then, soon after, they'd stagger out and into one of the dilapidated row houses at the bottom of San Francisco Street. There were always women standing around outside at the doorways to their houses and the boys would snicker and giggle at their red lips and painted faces as the men went in and out. There was something funny about the place, but the young boys could never quite put their finger on it. The older boys seemed to know, but they wouldn't ever divulge a thing, and wouldn't even let them tag along. Sunday evenings the

18

young trio would gather at the plaza to listen to the band concerts by Don Jose Amado Gutierrez and his band.

A few months after the wedding, the Antrim family left Santa Fe and moved to Silver City, where Mr. Antrim planned to work in the mines and Mrs. Antrim was to open a boardinghouse. He was a jack of all trades, preferring gambling, mining, and panning for gold in the streams up in the hills.

Contrary to his character, and being short of cash, however, he accepted a job in Knight's Butcher Shop shortly after their arrival in Silver City, but he very soon found out that the confining twelve hour days just weren't for him, and he soon resumed his mining ventures.

Young Catherine McCarty Antrim took sick, and a year and a half after her wedding she passed away. She developed what was known as consumption, mentioned by the Silver City newspaper, the "Mining Life" on September 19, 1874 as an "affection of the lungs."

The newspaper obituary read:

Died in Silver City, on Wednesday, the 16th inst. Catherine, wife of William Antrim, aged 34 years. Mrs. Antrim with her husband and family came to Silver City one year and a half ago, since which time her health has not been good, having suffered from an affection of the lungs, and for the last four months she has been confined to her bed. The funeral occurred from the family residence on Main Street, at 2 o'clock on Thursday.

Billy had been considerate and helpful to his mother during her illness, and his affection and kindness was well remembered by those who knew them. His grief was deep but controlled. Never again would he know the comforts of home or the loving care of a doting mother. His vagabond wanderings, which would characterize him for the last seven years of his short, turbulent life, were soon to begin.

After Catherine's death, William Antrim made one last futile attempt to keep the small family together, but was unsuccessful when Billy moved out a few days after his fifteenth birthday, while his brother Joseph went to Georgetown to work in the mines.

Billy, like most boys his age, had committed a few minor infractions, and had been sternly reprimanded by the law; afterwards, to his embarrassment, he had been punished by his stepfather. Angered, he moved into the Truesdell's Hotel, and was soon at work in the kitchen and dining room. His pay was free room and board, and occasionally a few cents on the side.

Years later, in his recollections, Mr. Truesdell would be quoted as saying that Billy was the only worker he ever had "who, never stole from me." This may have been true because he had befriended him after his mother's death, although Billy was never particularly known for his honesty. Many of his old acquaintances, however, were always ready to volunteer the information that, "Billy never stole from a friend." He stayed for a few months with the Truesdells, but by the middle of the summer cleaned out his room and left his job.

The hospitality of the humble Mexican people and their innate kindness and pity was almost all he needed for survival. All he had to do was be there "on time," like a homeless urchin, and he ate well.

"Arrimate, Beelee," they would say, "ven a comer." Then afterwards, among themselves they would say, "Como comen cinco, comen seis." Of course, he rotated his stopping places, as he did in later years when he suddenly "arrived" for a short visit, usually around dinnertime. He was not exactly a moocher, but he knew where to be at the right time, and who cooked the best *frijoles.*

From the Truesdells' Hotel, he moved to a room rented by the widow Brown, but being unemployed most of the time, he was lucky when he could come up with the rent. Such, it appears, was the case on this cold crisp day in October 1875, when he and his buddy Louie Abrahams were walking through Chinatown, their hands deep in their pockets, as one would walk on a cold day in October, or when one's pockets are absolutely, unquestionably empty.

"Wow," Billy exclaimed, when he saw the long line of

gleaming white shirts hanging in Sam Chung's backyard, drying in the sun. Chung and his partner Charley Sun operated the town's only laundry from their home on lower Bullard Street.

Billy immediately got the sharp idea of swiping the shirts and selling them to the secondhand dealer in old town; he knew he wouldn't ask too many questions, and would probably be delighted to get such good, clean merchandise for his smelly little store.

"Andale, Louie," he urged, and when Louie still held back, added disgustedly, "Bueno, culleperra si no vas," as he ran into the yard. Nobody, but nobody, in his right mind wanted to be *culleperra*, so Louie scrambled in, right behind him.

They swooped into the yard, quickly going down the line, snatching shirts right and left as fast as they could, and were close to the end of the line when out came Sam Chung, a basket of wet wash in his arms.

"Bandeets, bandeets," he called, as he took out after them, invoking all kinds of oriental anathemas over their heads, his hands waving frantically in the air.

The fleet-footed pair soon outdistanced him in the weed entanglements of the backyard arroyos, but Sam had a darned good idea who they were; he'd had plenty of trouble from the two before. They would run in the store, teasing him, singing such silly refrains as: *"Entre melon y melambe, mataron una ternera/Melon se comio la carne, y melambes la cagalera."* Sometimes they would say, "Y el Chino la cagalera," and he knew who "El Chino" was. He never knew quite what they meant, but he was wise enough to know it had to be something insulting or derogatory, so it made him mad.

He rushed off to see Marshall Givens, the veins pounding fiercely on his forehead. He was advised by the marshall to swear out a complaint against the pair, and he would gladly pick up the abusive young scoundrels. That evening, Billy was arrested by Sheriff Whitehall who admonished him quite forcefully for his crime, and promptly tossed him in the jail, "to rot," he said.

Billy was there for five long, wearisome days until the eve of his hearing before the judge, patiently awaiting a moment of carelessness on the part of his guard. When it came, he was ready to use the advantage to its fullest, and like a flash, disappeared out the window.

The newspaper account the following day said he had gone up the chimney. Regardless of what version was correct, however, the fact remains that he escaped; it was an escape which would lay the foundation for other more dangerous, more important escapes.

Billy had been non-complaining, co-operative and patient, but keenly observant and friendly, putting his guards at ease until the moment of his opportunity. Those variant qualities coupled with guts and mettle, he surmised, are what you need to have in this world if you expect to survive.

Swiftly, like an antelope at the snap of a twig, he bounded out the window, and in three noiseless leaps was gone, a blurred, indiscernible streak in the night.

He headed straight for the Truesdell home where he found Mrs. Truesdell knitting quietly by the fireside, her first fire of the early fall. When he told her what had happened, she reprimanded him gravely as she fed him and fixed up a bed for him for the night.

After all was quiet that night, she couldn't sleep for hours, pondering over the proper Christian course which she must take, and musing sadly over the dangerous trend Billy's life was taking. He wasn't really her responsibility after his mother's death last year, one part of her mind said—he's not even related. Yet, she finally resolved, it was her duty, her Christian duty, to use her influence and experience to help guide him as best she could.

She would talk to him first thing in the morning, she plotted, and with luck and God's help, she would convince him that he must turn himself in, face the music, and stop his delinquent behavior once and for all. Her conscience placated, she was soon able to sleep.

Her problems and plans were quickly resolved and put aside next morning, however, Billy was up before sunup and ready to leave. Anything she said, she well knew, would fall on dead ears. Resigning herself to his decision, she gave him some of her son's clothes and shoes, and whatever little money she could spare, and bade him farewell. She recited

22

one last prayer in his behalf, a worried frown on her face as she watched him depart in the early morning dark.

There was a small article that day in the *Grant County Herald* regarding the escape. She read it, shook her head sadly, and sighed.

> Henry McCarty, who was arrested on Thursday and committed to jail to await the action of the grand jury upon the charge of stealing clothes from Charley Sun and Sam Chung, celestials, sans coues, sans Joss sticks, escaped from prison yesterday through the chimney. It is believed that Henry was simply the tool of "Sombrero Jack," who done the stealing while Henry done the hiding, Jack has skinned out.

Sombrero Jack, it appears, was some poor, unfortunate, unappreciated derelict with bad habits, and the terms *san coues, Joss sticks*, etc. were obviously derogatory terms in vogue at the time, and used in rather bad taste. There were already thousands of Chinese people in the territory, and over the next four years, thousands more were to come into New Mexico and the West during the building of the railroads. Many of the Orientals were to settle down and remain.

Billy decided to flee towards the Arizona border where he felt he should be able to find refuge at the Knight Ranch. There just might be work at the ranch, he hoped, and he would be out of the sheriff's reach. Being young and immature, his mind probably exaggerated the importance of the crime he had committed and the penalties it could bring. Still, he no longer had anything in Silver City; his brother had gone back to Denver, his mother was dead, and he hadn't really liked his stepfather. He was ready to move on.

Visions of the tough, handsome cowboy he was going to be danced through his head. Unconsciously, his chest jutted out, and his shoulders appeared just a trifle bit broader as he ran through the back alleys on his way out of town.

A rooster crowed at the first signs of dawn; a dog barked and chased after him. He felt in his pocket for the buckboard fare which Mrs. Truesdell had generously helped him raise.

He waited under a tree at the outskirts of town and as the sun peeked over the mountain range to the east, he saw the buckboard round a bend in the road as it headed his way.

The driver was surprised when he rushed out and waved it down, but was relieved to see it was a mere boy. For a moment he had thought it was a highwayman and that he was about to be robbed. Billy paid his fare and was on his way. He never even looked back.

The dusty, rutted road, which in spots was more of a trail, headed west across the plains, barely skirting the northern reaches of the Burro Mountains. On two occasions, the two had to stop and fill small *arroyos* before they could continue on their way. The rains had cut deep swaths across the dry roadbed.

They crossed the Gila River which was not too high this time of year, and continued through the dust-laden trails along the west banks of the river until they reached the red rocks. To the right was the Knight ranch about fifteen miles away, the driver informed Billy as he stopped, but unfortunately he was heading in the opposite direction towards the ranches on down the river by the Pyramid Mountains.

It was late afternoon when they parted. As the buckboard rode off, Billy remembered the sack of apples Mrs. Truesdell had packed for him. He let out with a shrill, ear-bursting whistle and ran after the buckboard. As it stopped, Billy caught up to him and retrieved his bag, tossing the driver a big juicy red apple.

He started out on foot in the direction of the ranch, and as soon as he found a shady spot under a tree, he sat down to eat. He was hungry and tired, and joyfully thankful, when he realized that his benefactress had also included two large pieces of beef jerky in his sack.

What Billy didn't know as he headed for the knight Ranch, was that his friend Jesse Evans was wrangling at one of the ranches by the Pyramids where the buckboard driver was going.

Had he known this, that is where he would have gone, for Evans and he had been good friends when they'd lived in Silver City. As it was, he walked most of the night, finally stopping of to sleep when he could go no further. He huddled under a sharp rock outcropping, shivering in his light clothes all the long cold night which he thought would never end, trying to fall asleep. When morning finally came, he ran around jumping and clapping his hands together trying to warm up and get some circulation back into his cold, numb body. Finally, munching on an apple, he started out again.

The trail was getting narrower in spots, and sometimes completely disappeared when he realized that he was lost, and that this was no place for a wagon or a buckboard. He must have taken a wrong turn last night in the dark. Backtracking for what seemed like hours, he finally found where he had left the road on a curve and taken to the lightly traveled trail. Early that night he arrived at the ranch.

He was hired on the spot, as the Knights had to gather the stock and get ready for the long cold winter which would very soon be here. His pay, he found out, would be his grub, a place to sleep, and twenty dollars a month.

Even though the other ranch hands were very friendly, and he enjoyed the work, he wouldn't be here long, Billy planned; he hadn't even covered his tracks, just boarded the stage like a tourist on tour, and would be easy to find.

A ranch hand one day mentioned the whereabouts of his friend Jess Evans and all the money he'd heard they were making, "trading" in cattle and horses. He was at the first ranch at the northern edge of the Pyramids and was planning to ride out across the border to eastern Arizona where the pickings were even better. Billy collected his pay and was soon on his way on a borrowed horse. Jesse and gang were sure glad to see him and soon he was included in their plans.

The lack of excitement at the quiet little ranch gave the men little to do during off hours except fight and grumble. The pay on a ranch was too low, they griped, and there was no way you'd ever make a fortune unless you killed the owner and married the widow. They were soon moving on to greener pastures, they would always say.

One evening in the spring of '77 Bill and Evans headed further out west, Billy again on a borrowed horse, Evans on his own. As they neared the northern reaches of the Valle de Las Animas they saw an ominous looking cloud of dust in the valley below. They approached cautiously to see that it was exactly what they had expected—a band of Apache warriors getting ready to attack a small wagon train. The train was just circling into defensive formation when the war party attacked. The women and children ran to the center of the circle as the men loaded their guns and began firing.

With all their whooping and bloodcurdling screams, and being engulfed in a cloud of dust, the Indians didn't notice that Evans and Billy were picking them off from behind, one by one. When they finally realized it, they had lost many braves. Billy and Jesse continued their spirited battle, and when their ammunition ran out, they continued their siege with sharp knives and axes, finally routing the savages.

"After the party broke up," as Billy said, "We took their thank you's and appreciations and some grub they gratefully parted with and headed for the San Simon River and on west towards Fort Bowie."

What Billy failed to mention was that he also took his pick of the riderless Indian ponies and sent the borrowed horse back with a slap on the rump. They were still close by; he'd find his way back.

At Bowie they found things to their liking; the soldiers were bored and loved to gamble. Besides, what could this youngster, this kid, a barely visible peach fuzz of a beard grazing his cheeks, do? *"Que ha de hacer que mas valga,"* they laughed.

Billy was quick with cards and had learned a few tricks. He tried them all on them and was able to get by. He was quite a bluffer, studying their facial expressions, seeming always to pick the perfect time when the other's hand was weak, and so was able to rake in a few extra pots.

Another thing they liked about the fort was that there were always women there; some not too pretty, some not too young, and some not too clean—but women. They liked him too; he was so courteous, so mild and gentle, and yet so strong, every inch a man. His epicene, yet roguish appearance belied his manliness as it always would throughout his life.

His winnings kept them in liquor, women and grub for a while, but Billy's vagabond nature again won out. "Let's get the hell out of here, compadres," he said, and soon they were on the road again.

The next two years, 1877 and 1878, would prove to be the most exciting, most adventurous years for the kid. He was a full seventeen years old, tough, sharp and shrewd. These were to be his formative years.

Under the able tutelage of Jesse Evans he matured well. He was brave when bravery was called for, and swift when running was his best alternative. He always had a horse, and learned to ride it well, even though he was never known to have bought one. He never again would travel by buckboard.

His gun was the next most important possession of his life. He owned many, and lost many. His preference was a Colt .44 strapped to his hip, and a 44-40 Winchester rifle at his side. Since they both used the same size ammunition, he only had to carry the one type, and both guns were equally fast and reliable.

Where he acquired his guns was another thing. Some he bought, some were confiscated after a shooting, while others were picked up for "safekeeping" after a buddy's death. A man would much rather be caught without a mount or his pants just so long as his six-shooter was strapped to his side.

When a gun was destroyed or dropped during a skirmish, a man was completely lost without it as if he had lost his right arm. He would do anything until he had another, and soon the new one would fit the contours of his palm as if it had always belonged there. It was just a tool of his trade, but was treated with loving care, seeming to have a soul and personality all its own.

Up to now Billy had killed no white man; he had claimed his share of the raiding Apaches at Las Animas, but the year wouldn't end before he scratched a series of five or six notches on his gun. All white men.

In late July, 1877, the ruthless group ambushed three young Apache fur trappers in Apache Pass a few miles from old Fort Bowie in Arizona. After some time in the streams, the industrious young braves had half a dozen horses loaded with furs and pelts, their own mounts, guns and food. Well equipped and supplied, it appeared to them to be a good haul.

Billy, Jesse Evans, Melquiades Segura and their mysterious new partner, "Alias," together proceeded to annihilate the three young warriors. They never had a chance against the fearless, ferocious attack of the four desperadoes, and soon fell to their guns.

The victors gathered their loot, outfitting themselves with their victims' clothing, guns and supplies: the spoils of battle of the wild frontier.

After selling their ill-gained loot, Jesse Evans left the gang and rode out for the New Mexico Territory. He had heard tales about the big money to be made, and he wasn't going to let the golden opportunity pass him by.

There was some kind of a feud going on there. They were hiring men who could shoot and fight. "It was almost like a war," Evans said excitedly.

"These two men, Dolan and Murphy, would buy all the cattle you could rustle and they didn't care whose brand was on their rump." He continued, "You can make a fortune."

"Well," Billy said, "I'll probably follow later, but first I'd like to see some of the country down Mexico way, especially now that I have such a good guide in Segura, and maybe I'll even get to sample some of those beautiful señoritas he's always bragging about." Besides, he thought to himself, his eyes narrowing, he had a score to settle in Fort Grant before he left the Arizona Territory for good.

Chapter Two

Fort Grant And The Blacksmith

Billy and Evans had been to Fort Grant many times before while on their gambling circuit and knew the town well. This was where he had first met Gus Gildea, the scout, soon after his arrival from New Mexico, "bedecked in the Truesdell boy's Sunday clothes," he recalled grimly.

Most of Billy's first killings had been the aftermath of gambling arguments which had ended with both participants reaching for their guns, but this next one would be of a completely different nature.

On three different occasions, Billy had killed three gamblers: one in Tucson; one at Tombstone, the notorious mining camp twenty-five miles from the Mexican border; and another at some obscure army camp, perhaps Bowie, so he wasn't out of practice.

In what sequence the gambler killings had occured has faded into obscurity, but you can bet you boots that it wasn't that Billy was trying to rid the land of crooked gamblers per se; he just didn't like to be taken at cards.

The army post incident happened when he caught a Negro soldier cheating at poker. A violent quarrel followed, and when the solider tried to leave, Billy obligingly helped expedite his departure, a bullet hole in his chest.

Sometime after the gambler killings, Billy and his two pals rode out for Fort Grant. They had done plenty of gambling in this town too, together with lots of drinking and dancing at the saloons until the wee hours of the morning.

There would be no galavanting this time, however, as Billy had said, he had a score to settle. He was here to collect a gambling debt—or was it more to prove himself?

They entered George Adkins' Saloon, and were having some drinks when the town blacksmith, a blustery, breezy, bullheaded buffoon came in.

The two started arguing immediately, called each other a few vile names, and then—well, let's just read the account of a witness to the affair, given some years after.

The statement was made to *The Tucson Daily Citizen*, by Gus Gildea, Billys old friend, the scout and frontiersman, and appeared in its entirety in their issue of January 31, 1931.

It was in the fall of '77 when I first met "Billy the Kid." He was an easy going, likeable youth still in his teens. I was scouting at Fort Grant then, when Billy came to town, dressed like a "country jake," with store pants on and shoes instead of boots. He wore a six-shooter stuck in his trousers.

The blacksmith frequented George Adkins' saloon. He was called "Windy" because he was always blowing about first one thing then another. I don't recall the rest of his name. Shortly after the Kid came to Fort Grant, Windy started abusing him. He would throw Billy to the floor, ruffle his hair, slap his face, and humiliate him before the men in the saloon. Yes, the Kid was rather slender, with blue eyes and fair hair. The blacksmith was a large man, with a gruff voice and manner. One day he threw the youth to the floor, pinned his arms down with his knees and started slapping his face.

"You are hurting me—let me up," cried the Kid. "I want to hurt you, that's why I got you down," was the reply.

People in the saloon watched the two on the floor. Billy's right arm was free from the elbow down. He started working his hand around and finally managed to

30

grasp his .45.

Suddenly, silence reigned in the room. The black-smith evidently felt the pistol against his side, for he straightened slightly. Then there was a deafening roar. Windy slumped to the side as the Kid squirmed free and ran to the door, vaulted into the saddle on John Murphy's racing pony, and left Fort Grant.

When I came to town the next day from Hooker's Ranch where I was working then, Murphy was storming and cursing the Kid, calling him a horse thief, murderer and similiar names. I told him he would get his horse back, for the Kid was no thief.

In about a week one of Murphy's friends rode into town on Cashaw, Murphy's horse, saying the Kid had asked him to return the animal to the owner.

This, in all appearances, was the famous tragic killing of "the blacksmith who insulted Billy's mother." She had been dead for almost three years. Of course, in his cursing, Windy just may have insulted his mother in absentia. Who knows?

E.P. "Windy" Cahil didn't die until the next day, August 18, 1877, and was able to make a statement to the effect that he had had some trouble with Antrim before the shooting. The news story in *The Arizona Citizen* of August 22nd, confirmed the story:

Austin Antrim shot E.P. Cahil near Fort Grant on the 17th inst. and the latter died on the 18th. Cahil made a statement before his death to the effect that he had had some trouble with Antrim during which the shooting was done. Deceased had a sister, Margaret Flanegan, in Cambridge, Massachusetts, and another, Kate Conlon, in San Francisco. He was born in Galway, Ireland, and was aged thirty-two. The coroners jury found that: "The shooting was criminal and unjustifiable, and that Henry Antrim, alias Kid, is guilty thereof." The inquest was held by M.L. Wood, J.P., and the jurors were M. McDowell, George Teaque, T. McCleary, D.M. Norton, Jas. L. Hunt, and D.H. Smith.

31

Even though the article first mentioned him as Austin, it is obvious as we read further, who they were talking about. The same article was picked up by the *Grant County Herald* on September 1, 1877, adding that "bad names were applied to each other."

The trio headed east, across Turkey Flats, stopping off at the San Simon River to water their horses and fill their canteens. After resting a bit, they ambled downstream for about a mile to obliterate their tracks, emerging on a grassy knoll on the east bank of the river, and headed over the dry plains towards the safety of the Piloncillo Mountains.

Billy was still riding John Murphy's racing steed. He would have liked to keep the beautiful swift animal for himself, but he would not even consider it. He knew John Murphy, the owner, and to Billy's strange way of reasoning, this made all the difference—he wouldn't steal from a friend.

His own horse, it appears, had been confiscated after the shooting in Fort Grant, and he would probably never see it again. Well, easy come, easy go; it had most likely belonged to one of the unfortunate Indian trappers they had annihilated by the Chiricaquas at Apache Pass, thirty-five miles down the San Simon.

They camped that night at the base of the Piloncillos, in the area between the majestic twin peaks, and the next day continued east to the Gila River and on up into the Burro Mountains. This was the same ranch area that Jesse Evans was working in when Billy had arrived at the Knight Ranch over a year before.

The Mesilla Daily Independent's article of September 17th, 1877, heralded their arrival back in the territory, accusing them of horse theft:

> On Monday last, three horses belonging respectively to Colonel Ledbetter, John Swishelm and Mendoza, were stolen from Pass Coal Camp in the Burro Mountains. On learning the fact, Colonel Ledbetter and Swishelm went out to the camp and trailed them in on the road at Apache Tahoe. Sometimes on Tuesday the party of thieves, among whom was Henry Antrim, were met at Cook's Canyon by Mr. Carpenter. Telegrams have

32

been sent to Sheriff Barela at Mesilla, and we hope to hear of the arrest of the thieves and recovery of the horses.

Billy needed a new horse; he had sent John Murphy's back, so it is quite possible that he had pulled off this latest theft, and he *was* in the area.

If he was caught, Billy reasoned, he would probably be sent back to Fort Grant and tried for Windy Cahil's killing. He envisioned himself dangling at the end of a rope, kicking and gasping for breath, and he didn't like one bit what he saw. Now was the time to take Melquiade's exhortation seriously and pay a visit to the beautiful, dark haired Señoritas south of the border.

Through the dry, cactus studded plains they fled towards the Mexican border a hundred miles away, always heading straight south. Five days later they were in the State of Sonora, and the sleepy village of Aguas Prietas. It was an old village with dusty, narrow streets which were more like trails, zigzagging haphazardly in between the brown adobe houses. The broiling sun beat down continuously, but when the miracle of rain occurred, they became sticky, muddy caliche bogs out of which even the horses had a difficult time trying to escape.

The natives were a quiet and peaceful lot, with few if any ambitions. During the hotter parts of the day they disappeared from the streets altogether, taking to their cool, naturally insulated adobe huts for a noon rest. As the sun beat down unmercifully, it seemed to affect everyone; the more you slept, the more you wanted to sleep, making a man slow and lazy and completely apathetic. The only place with any life, of course, was in the cantinas. The *aguardiente*, and half warm *cerveza* gave everyone there a completely different perspective from those outside.

Billy and Melquiades arrived in mid-afternoon, gazing around languidly at the unobtrusive surroundings. They walked down the road, leading their horses, perspiration rolling down their cheeks. Alias, the mysterious, unknown partner, following uncommunicably a few yards behind.

"Va a bailar La Trola," someone hollered enthusiastically

out the door of the cantina as the trio approached. Outside, in the shade, some men laughed foolishly at the announcement. "Es que va a bailar la Trola," they repeated.

The cantina was filled with gaiety and laughter as men left their tables and high-perched stools, descending on a small platform in the corner of the room, their beers in their hands. La Trola was drunkenly making her way to the stage: she was a short, fat, overly made-up caricature of a woman, the men's cheers and banter egging her on. The band, which consisted of two half-tipsy guitarists, one with an instrument with only four strings, so old and battered it looked as if it was about to fall apart, started to play.

A sallow-faced man hicupped loudly, and with a look of utter surprise, slapped his palm to his mouth and ran haphazardly between the tables to the back of the room, never quite making it out the back door.

"Limpia lo, cabron," someone said disgustedly.

La Trola started to shake and shimmy, every bit of her enormous bulk in motion at once, shaking the corner of the room like an earthquake. Her great breasts, braless under her tight, shiny dress, shaking first to the right, then to the left, then straight up and down, momentarily hypnotized and quieted the gaping men.

Suddenly, they woke up, whooping and hollering as she seductively lowered the frayed strap on her dirty red dress. It had been down most of the day, and nobody'd noticed, but now the mere gesture made them shout with excitement.

The music ended rather abruptly, with two last, sharp scrapes of the guitars, and everyone started back to his seat amidst poignant, rancid smells of stale underarms and what the pale-faced man was trying to clean up on the floor in the back. La Trola, perspiration pouring out of her every pore, tiredly trodded back to her table, already forgotten even before the men returned to their seats.

In the other corner of the room, a serious-looking group never even raised their heads, never even appeared to have heard the din and commotion or seen the lively, drunken spectacle in the corner. They were playing Monte, an ageless game of chance, of addicting propensities and obscure origin. This was where Billy and Melquiades directed their attention.

34

The surly gamesters never looked up as the pair approached the table, dark brown, cloudy, lukewarm beers in their hands.

"Buenas tardes, amigos," Billy said, smiling. "Podemos entrarle al juego?" ("May we join in?")

Startled, everyone looked up at Billy's ruddy, weather-tanned, friendly, smiling face, two upper teeth protruding slightly.

"Quien es este gringito atrevido," they thought. (Who speaks our tongue as well or better than us?)

They saw a young man, a beer in his left hand, both hands on his hips, relaxed stance, cocky and challenging, a gun in his holster, wearing a big hat and boots, ruddy complexioned, tanned face, dusty peeling nose under warm blue-green eyes speckled with brown, sincere, straightforward, and sure of himself.

"Arrimate," a leader type said gruffly, happy he didn't have to respond in English. As he proceeded to explain the rules of the game, limits and raises, Billy, half listening, was thinking to himself that Melquiades and he made good partners; they were equally fluent in the Spanish language, were good fighters and good gamblers. They should do well in Mexico together. Billy had no idea that his stay in the village would be of very short duration. In a short while, they would be scrambling hastily to get out of town. The reason? The same monte dealer who had allowed him to play, and was just now seated across the table from him. Billy's itchy trigger finger would soon dispatch the man, whose name was Jose Martinez, to his maker, after the usual argument over cards.

The trio would flee that night, right after the shooting, towards the high Sierra Madres in the southern reaches of the Pyramid chain, and since everything they owned was already packed and on their horses, there was nothing in Aguas Prietas to hold them back. They sped through the dark that night, with no chance to stop off and rest on the way, a posse of Mexicans closely in pursuit. They followed the trio practically on their heels, through the hills and gullies and dry arroyo beds for over ten days, but were never able to catch up to them.

After a few days the unsuccessful posse gave up and

returned to Sonora, and even though a substantial reward was offered by the influential Martinez family for their capture, it was never collected. The people soon settled back down to their old quiet, peaceful ways and forgot the incident.

El Bilito was too fast and too sly, they concluded, and besides, hadn't Don Jose asked for it? "Solo busco su ruina." ("He sought his own ruin") they would say.

It seems that Don Jose had taken an instant disliking to Billy, with constant obvious references to "cabrones gringos Tejanos," coupled with lengthy tirades as to why in blazes they didn't stay where they belonged? Quite often he held back money that Billy had won, and on one such an occasion he finally got Billy's goat.

"Are you as fast with your pistol as you are with your tongue?" Billy asked. Instantly, both their shots rang out as one, and Martinez slowly slid under the table; his partners disappeared from his side in a flash, each going his own way, and Billy and Segura, quickly vaulted into their saddles and faded into the night. Alias was right behind!

Laughing at their latest escapade, they again headed for the High Sierras, and late that night made camp by a cool mountain stream, Billy nursing a bullet burn on his cheek. They ate the dried mutton jerky and dark tortillas they had bought in Aguas Prietas, without benefit of a campfire, and as they wearily untied their blankets from their horses, they made plans for the next day.

Over the mountains lay el Estado de Chihuahua and Cuidad Chihuahua itself, Melquiades said, "and even more beautiful Señoritas than those in Aguas Prietas." It was much larger than those measly little villages they had been plucking so far, and the pickings were rumored to be exceptionally good. Besides, they should be able to lose themselves much more easily there, and would be safe from the relatives of Don Jose, may he rest in peace. Not that they were afraid of them, but you always had to be prepared.

"El que para la oreja, no tiene queja," Billy said, a Spanish version of "Be Prepared."

They arrived in Cuidad Chihuahua next day about noon, and immediately headed for the baths. They had plenty of pesos and pesetas with them now. It seems that as Martinez had slid quietly to the floor at Aguas Prietas, Billy not one to lose an opportunity, had grabbed his share of the wealth off the table in the turmoil and excitment before running out the door. They were dusty and dirty, and itching with brush vermin, but before they got into the tubs, they found an old lady, black tapalo pressed tightly to her brow, who would be glad to wash and iron their clothes for a few pesos, and who was heartily recommended to them by the owner of the hotel.

By late afternoon the hot Chihuahua sun had done its job well, and so had the little old lady. They dressed up in their clean, fresh duds and went out into the streets. The rest in real beds with soft mattresses and the fine hot dinner of burriñates con frijoles and chile con queso de cabra at the hotel, had gotten them in the perfect mood for a good game of cards. They picked the one that looked most promising, but it was soon obvious to them that they were not wanted and were not welcome. The veiled hatred and envy, perhaps over Billy's gambling prowess, were never absent. They went from one place to the other over the next few days, winning in all.

Even though they didn't call him a "gringo Tejano," he knew it was on the tip of their tongue. Even though he spoke their language well and tried to be friendly, he was never quite made at ease—they just didn't want *gringos* around.

One night he had been winning constantly at monte, when it came time for the dealer to pay him at the end of one round, he refused, saying that the bank had just gone broke, all the while raking in pots from the other players and into his dealer's bag.

"Andele," Billy said, "pagueme, yo le gane, hay tiene con que." The gambler ignored him. For a few seconds Billy looked him straight in the eyes with a mean, murderous glare, turned on his heel and stalked out.

That night the monte dealer who had made the biggest mistake of his life, disappeared while on his way home in the early hours of the morning. Neither he nor his little leather money bag was ever seen again. Other dealers who had been unfriendly or insulting also parted with their little bags that night. Billy had gotten his revenge.

37

In the warm, moonlit autumn night they fled towards El Rio Grande. They had lost "Alias" in their latest skirmish, and looked back often, expecting him to catch up to them soon, but he never did. They never heard from him again.

Upon reaching Juarez, Mexico the friends of many an adventure parted. Billy was going north to La Mesilla where he felt he might meet up with Jesse Evans and a respectable ranch job, and Segura wanted to visit the home of his parents at San Elizario, Texas about twenty-five miles south of Paso del Norte, where he was born. After a hearty handshake and a couple of slaps on the back they parted.

"Adios amigo", Billy said.

"Adios amigo, valla con Dios," Segura responded, even though neither one of them had exactly been, "con Dios," (with God) for quite a spell.

Billy was at a small ranch about six miles northwest of La Mesilla a few days later when he met up with Evans and some cowboy friends he had teamed up with on a sojourn to Las Cruces. His new partners were Frank Baker, William Morton and James McDaniels. Enthusiastically the gang invited Billy to join forces with them on the Rio Pecos in the area of the Seven Rivers, about one hundred and fifty miles to the east. They guaranteed Billy that he would have plenty to do with an exceptionally good return and, "You sure as 'el won't be bored," Evans added loudly, bringing chuckles and knowing looks from his cohorts.

Quickly convinced, Billy eagerly agreed to join them, and they all shook hands on the deal. He would see them in a few days, he said, as soon as he settled his affairs in Las Cruces and contacted a friend, Segura, whom he was sure would want to go along too. Billy immediately sent a communication to Segura at San Elizario telling him about the good opportunities in the Pecos River area and advising him that he would wait for him in Mesilla and they would cross the desert together. Segura quickly sent him a positive response, and started to get his belongings together for the trip.

Billy waited patiently for many days for his friend's arrival, but he never came. Finally a few days later, tired of waiting, he was at the ranch close to Mesilla getting set to leave, when a young Mexican boy arrived with a message. Segura had been arrested in San Elizario and there was angry talk by the citizens of holding a necktie party in his honor. What crime he had been charged with was not mentioned but quite possibly their communications may have been intercepted and read. The news of their notoriety had surely reached the ears of Segura's paisanos by this time.

Segura had been a good companion, Billy thought; he had liked his easygoing, friendly ways. They had had many enjoyable times and many an exciting adventure together. Now he was in trouble, deep trouble it appeared from the message he'd received. He took the folded piece of paper from his pocket and read it again, crumpling it in his fist. "Vaya a la Madre," he said loudly as he jumped up. No way was he going to stand idly by and let them hang his good friend, Melquiades. Now spurred into action, he made hasty plans. He could be at Elizario before daybreak he figured, and wasn't that the best time to perpetrate an effective jailbreak? He would do it. It was to be an astonishing ride and hailed by folklore in the same way as Paul Revere's ride and the message to Garcia.

That afternoon he readied his horse for the daring ride. He fed it early on oats and crushed corn and allowed it only a few short drinks of water before they were on their way. He didn't want it to be lazy and bloated. The road to Paso del Norte on the sleepy Rio Grande was straight and well traveled, so he was able to make the fifty-five miles by midnight. Shortly thereafter, he crossed the river and continued south on the Mexico-Texas border, and by about three o'clock in the morning was in San Elizario. He stopped in the outskirts of the town and let his snorting, sweating horse rest a bit and catch its breath; then quietly as a phantom, he stole through the sleeping town to the jail on foot, leading his horse. He knocked loudly on the heavy wooden door, waking up one of the Mexican deputies guarding the prisoner.

"Quien es?" he asked.

"Texas Rangers," Billy answered, then in Spanish, "Traimos dos Americanos." ("We have two American prisoners.")

39

Cautiously, the guard opened the door and peered out, only to find himself face to face with Billy's .44 revolver. Billy shoved it in his gullet, warning him not to make a sound. The guard immediately put up his hands, and with a trembling voice assured him that he had absolutely no intentions of attempting bravery.

Billy was fumbling with the keys, searching for the right one to Melquiades' cell. "Qual es?" he had asked, when the other guard walked in from the backroom yawning. Startled and in the act of stretching his limbs, he obviously had no intention of playing the hero either, Billy figured, as he relieved him of his gun.

After locating the proper key, he released Segura, who was overjoyed to see his brave compadre, and ordered the two jailers into his cell. Locking the steel door behind them, he tossed the keys outside into the weeds. At breakneck speed, they fled San Elizario that brisk September morning, heading for the sanctuary of Mexico across the river. No great obstacle, they easily crossed the river, and skirting nopales, in a short while were knocking at a friend's door a short distance from Guadalupe. They holed up here for a few days until they were sure they had not been followed. Since at times there was a semblance of cooperation between law enforcement bodies on both sides of the border they couldn't be too careful—this could be just such a time. The two parted here. Segura, fearing the noose, decided to make his way further south into the interior and lose himself in the vast Mexican territory. He disappeared into obscurity and Billy never heard from him again.

His thoughts once again turning to his long delayed trek to the Seven Rivers country by the Pecos, Billy decided to return to La Mesilla first and leave from there. While leaving town next day, he met up with Tom O'Keefe, a long time friend of Evans, and after a bit of convincing, they joined forces for the long trip east. O'Keefe, like Billy, was not quite eighteen; a handsome, virile young cowboy always searching for adventure. With Billy he would find more than he had bargained for.

Their destination, the Valley of the Seven Rivers, is about a hundred and forty miles straight east from Mesilla as the crow flies, at least a hundred of them a desolate stretch of desert. The valley is named for its many tributaries, each of them flowing east into the Pecos. They are the Rio Feliz, (Happy River); Rio Hondo, (Deep River); Rio Penasco (Rocky River); Rio Bonito (Pretty River); Rio Salado (Salty River); and the Pecos.

Since it was late in the fall, Billy reasoned, it would not be quite as hard a crossing as in the heat of midsummer so they should be able to make good time. They would travel mostly at night and in the early evening hours, finding a shady spot through the hotter parts of the day to rest the horses and catch some sleep. The trip was easy and uneventful until the second day. They had reached the western slope of the Guadalupe Mountains and had started to cross over the divide when they were attacked by Indian warriors. Billy had been warned by Evans not to attempt the crossing at the high mountain pass in the Guadalupes since the area was thoroughly infested with hostile Apaches; but the warning, and the ever-present thought of adventure had only served to spur him on. Besides, the thought of going north all around the Sacramento Mountains through the trail and to the Rio Penasco then back east to the Pecos only because of fear was not very appealing to him. It would add another fifty or sixty miles to their journey.

"No," Billy said, "we're heading straight east, we won't ask for no trouble, but if it just happens that they're ahankering for some action, we'll give them back a taste of their own medicine and then some."

Tom and Billy had seen plenty of Indian signs once they had neared the base of the Guadalupes. A well-worn trail, full of fresh unshod horse tracks seemed headed towards the craggy red bluffs Billy had been told housed a fresh water spring. His dry tongue licked his cracked parched lips at the thought.

Tom wanted to wait until they were sure that the Indians had left the spring or even bypass the area altogether, but the lure of a thirst-quenching drink of ice cold water, and refilling their fast-dwindling supply with perhaps even a quick cool dip in its pool afterwards, was just too tempting to them both to pass up.

Billy left his horse and their burro loaded with supplies with Tom, then crouching down low, crept stealthily on foot forward, scouting the area up ahead. The trail led straight to the pass, a patch of sky in the distance showing its emergence point on the other side.

The pass narrowed sharply, almost down to shoulder width. Billy listened. There was no sound except his own heavy panting. Too quiet; something was wrong. He sensed it and knew it—his nose smelled it—his very bones told him there was danger up ahead, yet inborn stubbornness and determination made him inch on.

Now he heard something. He cocked his ear; there was a soft gurgling sound. It was the spring, he thought, as he peeked around the red clay banks to his left. He had just caught sight of the radiantly green oasis, a verdant spectrum in the desert, beckoning, its bubbly waters incandescently sparkling in the sun. He had just relaxed his shoulders, his life-hardened eyes hungrily devouring its exquisitely resplendent beauty, when suddenly a scream right up above his head shattered the peaceful moment. A cloud of dust billowed up; a blood-curdling Indian war whoop made him jump straight up a foot, every hair on his head standing on end. He squashed his hat down, hiked his pants and in the same motion cocked his gun and shot straight up; a screaming savage tumbled down the ledge and rolled to a stop at his feet.

He didn't wait to see if he were dead. He jumped over him, and with great speed reversed directions and fled out of the crag the way that he had come, half-expecting an arrow to plow through his shoulder blades at any moment.

"Get your ass moving," he hollered at O'Keefe, referring to the donkey loaded with supplies. "And the horses," he added as an afterthought. He ran up the steep cliffside and started to climb. He knew he'd never make it to his horse, and it would be an easy thing for them to pick him off in the scrub or play cat and mouse with him around the Piñones.

Quickly sensing his dilemma, he struggled up the cliff, accidently rolling a boulder in his wake. He looked back to see his pursuers scrambling hastily to get out of its way.

"Wow," he hollered, "what a weapon."

Arrows, together with choice Apache curses rained all

around him, punctuated by bullets. He scurried to get out of their range. As one brave stood up clumsily to raise his rifle, Billy expertly deposited a hot lead ball right between his eyes. His foot purposely pushed on another big red boulder, dislodging it, until with a roar, it too tumbled down the canyon wall. He whooped and hollered with laughter as he watched the braves scamper to get out of its way—some of them didn't make it.

He had wanted to laugh when his hair stood up on end a little while before. He had wondered at the time who had scared the other the worse when they'd met up in the crag—the Indian or him. His laughter could be heard clear across the valley now as he sat down in the dirt and whacked the ground with his hat; two little jagged paths of tears rolled down his cheeks. Choking and coughing he tried to regain control. "Better straighten up," he told himself, sobering up fast, "before I get an arrow in my scalp." He wiped the tears off roughly with the back of his hand, smudging his face. Once again he was alert, serious—the humorous incident gone from his mind, saved, to be recounted often in campfire braggadocio in years to come.

His pursuers, instead of climbing, seemed to be dispersing. They had had a minor powwow and now were retrieving their horses and ambling off, one by one. Perhaps they too had glimpsed the humor in the situation, or admired the courage of this laughing, red-faced, daredevil white boy, but whatever it was, they left and they didn't come back.

Not trusting them and half expecting them to go around and come up the mountain on the other side above him to start rolling boulders down, Billy decided to make haste. Along the rattlesnake-infested base of the cliff he went, half running, half sliding until he felt he was far enough away and had lost himself from them quite completely.

Exhausted he rested awhile, then went on. Late in the evening he sat and rested on a ledge on the eastern slope of the mountain, and only then did he stop to think and wonder about his partner O'Keefe. He had the horses and donkey loaded with grub, so if the Indians didn't get him, he was in better shape than Billy. They would meet up in the Pecos River country, he figured, if he could ever find his own way there. From the ledge he charted the way in his mind to the best of his ability. It appeared to him that he should cross that valley, and continue in a straight line east—if that was east over there.

Exhausted, he nestled down in a bed of leaves under a protective, brushy tree and slept. Not even the night-long howling of the coyotes would wake him up tonight. But what the howling coyotes couldn't accomplish the early morning dew and its penetrating cold took care of instantly. He awoke shivering in his light clothes as the first streaks of dawn showed in the skies to the east. Now he knew which way was east, a fact the sun couldn't hide. By sunrise he was slowly making his way down the northeast side of the Guadalupe Pass.

For the next three days he walked, always towards the rising sun, sleeping in semiprotected arroyos and gullies, eating wild teosinte grass or whatever other rare edible vegetation he recognized, and finally, weatherbeaten, hungry and exhausted, he stumbled into one of the many range camps by the Pecos.

Jesse Evans soon heard of his whereabouts, and a few days later the Kid, fed, rested and recuperated, chatted with him excitedly of his adventures by the campfire.

"Well," Evans said, "if you're ever going to get started with us, now is as good a time as any," and Billy agreed. His easy recruitment into the services of Murphy and Dolan was perhaps made easier by the fact that Billy had no horse, no rifle or ammunition for his six-shooter which he had somehow managed to keep by his side, and soon after was completely outfitted for the tasks to come.

Before starting his new association, Billy had expressed the desire to learn the whereabouts of his friend O'Keefe, so with a couple of new-found friends he had made the trip back to Mesilla. Whatever route he chose this time we do not know. Perhaps it was less exciting, but in due time he found O'Keefe alive and well in Las Cruces.

The repentant young fighter told his version of the adventure story after the Indian attack, and his trip back to civilization. "The horses and loaded burro got spooked when the shooting and yelling started," O'Keefe said, "and I had to walk most of the way back to La Mesilla."

Before leaving the battle area, however, he had caught sight of Billy climbing the steep hills almost a mile away, and had heard his uncontrollable laughter reverberating through the valley. He figured he had gone loco. Who wouldn't, with a hundred Indians after you? He had reasoned solemnly. He had hidden in a rocky crevice nearby, and late that night by the light of the moon, had stolen undetected to the much sought water hole, drank up, filled his canteen, and bade farewell to this Godforsaken land. After having walked a great distance, he had quite unexpectedly caught sight of his horse standing alone and forlorn in the middle of the prairie. He rounded him up easily, and had made it back to civilization in about two days.

Billy urged him to ride back to the Pecos with them, enticing him with stories of the ease with which he had found good interesting work, but O'Keefe would hear nothing of it. He had had enough. He didn't care if he never even saw the Guadalupes again, and had absolutely no intentions of even riding that territory in the future. Then, Billy left him, content in the knowledge that he was alive and safe, and a few days later was seen riding with his friends into one of Evan's hideouts in a little ranch by the rolling Pecos River.

Throughout the fall and winter of '77, the Evans gang or the "Seven Rivers Warriors" as they liked to be known, occupied themselves rustling cattle, always finding a ready market with their customers, no questions asked. They, in turn, had valuable U.S. Government and U.S. Army contracts to fulfill. Besides the soldiers at the forts, the government had thousands of Indians on the reservations as its personal responsibility. The maligned ranchers were up in arms. They were offering big rewards for the capture of the Evans gang, but like the proverbial cat of nine lives they eluded their clutches time after time.

Since the early 1870's, outlaws from all over the southwest had been converging on the lawless Lincoln County area. They found there many things to their liking; a 25,000-square-mile refuge in which to ply their trade, the pock-marked Guadalupe Mountains, with their ideal natural hideouts, abundant game and clear water springs, and above all, hundreds of loose, wild mavericks roaming the range.

As an added bonus they had the *bailes* in the Placitas; the beautiful, lively señoritas, with pearly white teeth and dark star-studded eyes, and plenty of *aguardiente* and *cerveza*. All a young cowboy had to do was keep señor Murphy well-supplied with beef at five dollars a head, and he could live high off the hog.

The civil strife which for years had been smouldering among the cattle barons and their hired gunmen was about to burst into flames. The feud which Evans had mentioned in Mesilla appeared to have been understated. There was a new incident born every day, soon to be repaid by a like atrocity. Night riders were on the move and once a man took sides he risked life and limb, family and possessions. The friendly Mexicans who had originally settled the valleys were for the first time bolting their doors. Up and down the county one saw nothing but apprehension and unrest. Such was the situation in Lincoln County, which the adventurous Bilito was introduced into in the fall of 1877, shortly before his eighteenth birthday.

Chapter Three

The Lincoln County Troubles

The Lincoln County area in the beautiful southeastern corner of New Mexico has been inhabited continuously for thousands of years. Its many rivers and fertile valleys have provided water, forage and ideal living conditions for the thundering buffalo herds and deer, and respite for the tired wandering plains Indians for unknown ages. Before the United States occupation in 1846 its *llanos* and *valles* and high peaked mountaintops had been the vast free domain of hostile nomadic Indian tribes.

Its horizons, as far as the eye could see in any direction, was home for the ancient Apache, Wemenuche Ute, and Comanche Indian cultures. Under the leadership of great chiefs such as Nana, Victorio, Persechopa, Roman, Geronimo, San Pablo, Caballero Gonzalez, San Juan, and nameless others, the Indians had fought the white man throughout the southwest, and had even attempted to live in peace with him, but the continuous depredations and injustices commited against them by the greedy white man had never permitted them rest. Little by little they had been pushed out, first by the Spanish and Mexican encroachments on their territory and now by the land-grabbing, claim-staking white man. Their vast, open plains had never before seen this strange separating and splitting of the land into parcels of private ownership as was now being done. No one could own the land, they reasoned with the timeless naivety of their ancestors; it was there for the deer, the elk, the antelope, and the buffalo, and for the people to live on, hunt, and enjoy. It belonged to no one; it belonged to all. But their way of life, like a wisp in the breeze, would soon be gone forever; it was of the past, never again to be. Their customs were to be forgotten, their culture to lie in shambles.

They were driven from their lands, their villages and pueblos, pillaged and plundered, then burned, their families raped, scattered, and murdered. They were rounded up like cattle, and herded into strategically located Indian reservations. The largest of them all was the Mescalero Apache Indian Reservation. South of Fort Stanton in Lincoln County, it was established by government decree on May 29, 1873. Its boundaries according to the *Las Vegas Gazette* of July 3, 1873 were as follows:

> Commencing at the southwest corner of the Fort Stanton reduced military reservation and running thence due south to a point on the hills near the north bank of the Rio Ruidoso, thence along said hills to a point above the settlements, thence across said river to a point on the hills, thence to the same line upon which we start from Fort Stanton, and thence due south to the 33rd degree of north latitude; thence to the top of the Sacramento Mountains and along the top of said mountains to the headwaters of the Rio Nogal, thence to a point—an enormous range of useless arid dry land.

That the Indians were not content in their new habitat was obvious to many since the beginning.

In an attempt to bring the Jicarilla Apaches into the fold, and in the process acquire their vast fertile lands, the government officials had offered them many inducements and had painted a very rosy picture of the reservation. It was not to be believed!

San Pablo, the head chief of the Jicarillas, had made the long trip to Fort Stanton and had come back unconvinced and disillusioned. On his return to Cimarron he had been interviewed by the *Cimarron News and Press*. Their article which also appeared verbatim in the *Santa Fe New Mexican* of May 10, 1879, follows:

> San Pablo the head chief of the Jicarilla Apaches, who left here last year for the reservation near Fort Stanton, (Mescalero) paid Cimmaron a visit last Saturday and Sunday. He says that he remained on the Stanton reservation but two weeks; that the country was not the way it was represented to his people, and that the few who accompanied him there were dissatisfied, and would prefer to depend upon their guns for subsistence rather than to draw rations at that point. He stated that his people were scattered all through the mountains west of Cimarron, and that they would go down into the buffalo country soon.

Even though many of the tribes crowded into the reservation had been farmers, the majority preferred to live off of the plentiful wild game in the forests and the native plants and shrubs, of which every use, edible or medicinal, had been known by them for ages. The majority preferred their old nomadic way of life; preferred their freedom, of course, to captivity. They no longer had any choice.

At this time, the Indians' circumstances were not very pleasant; the plight of the proud Jicarilla, Gila, and Mescalero Apaches, the Utes and the Commanches was in an uncomfortable, unhappy state of affairs.

A few white men sympathized with the Indians and did their best to alleviate their pitiful cause. Champion among them was Albert J. Fountain, who in a letter to *The New York Sun* on May 4, 1880, expressed the ever-present fear and danger of a new Indian uprising, blaming the violent, inhuman acts committed against them by the white settlers and the flagrant fiscal mismanagement by the agents on Indian affairs. His letter also appeared in the *Las Vegas Gazette* of May 9, 1880:

I start tonight for the Mescalero Apache Indian Reservation. They are having a terrible time over there. General Hatch, after having been whipped all over the country by Victorio, has gone to the Mescalero agency and driven off all the Indians who were behaving themselves. My old friends, Caballero Gonzales and San Juan, the principal chiefs of the Mescaleros, have fled from the reservation, and it is feared that they will take to the warpath. I am sent for to go out and try to induce them to return. The whole country east of us is up in arms. Victorio with not less than two hundred warriors has whipped over eight hundred troops. A battle occurred a few days ago in which there were four hundred troops and not over sixty Indians under Nana. The troops claimed a victory and pretended that they had killed Indians when in fact they were badly defeated, and came near being annihilated. They lost one captain and seven men, and killed one squaw, and General Hatch makes a big blow about it in the papers, and claims a great victory. I predicted this thing months ago. Of all the wretched mismanagement which uniformly characterizes the conduct of Indian affairs on this frontier, there has been none equal to this last, and I feel that hundreds of lives will be sacrificed by the imbecility and criminal stupidity of all our officials.

The sentiments of Mr. Fountain were not his own alone, but were widespread among thinking people of all races.

The big cattle barons from the bordering Texas panhandle had come in, claiming thousands of acres of public lands as their own, further enhancing the sorry predicament of the proud Indian tribes, but unfortunately they were here to stay. They were strong and powerful, with the full backing of the United States Army, their own guns, and fearless cowboys; eventually their debilitated oppressed opposition dwindled and died.

Hurt also by the actions of the big cattle kings were the small ranchers, both white and Mexican. Their herds were often lost, carried away in the massive, thunderous roundups of the ruthless cattle barons and their gigantic herds. Having acquired large government contracts to supply the reservations and the U.S. Army to boot, the cattle business was thriving. With the coming of the railroad in 1879, they now had access to the lucrative markets to the north, east, and further west as far as the Pacific.

Since about 1867 when John Chisum and his band of young cowboys came over the Texas-New Mexico border, driving before them thousands of head of Texas longhorns, there had been rumblings of trouble among the natives and ranchers, but still, over the Llano Stacado, into the valley of the Pecos River they came, spreading his powerful name. He laid claim to thousands of acres of prime grazing land formerly Comanche territory, and from there built his great empire. From old Fort Sumner to Pecos, Texas he was king, his sphere of influence encompassing an area of over two hundred miles long and sixty miles wide; over twenty-five thousand square miles altogether. At one time, his ranch was home for over one hundred thousand head of half wild, full-blooded Texas longhorns, the "Jingle Bob" and "Long Bar" brand as their mark. The brands were his own idea. The first was simply a long bar brand running almost the length of the steer, and the Jingle Bob was a sharp knife slit in each ear, so that the lower part of the animal's ear would curl and hang, and the upper part would point straight up. Proud of his invention, only a few expert craftsmen were permitted to do one, because it was easy to botch up the job. It would leave either both parts of the ear drooping or both parts pointing straight up. Easily recognized and effective, the Jingle Bob was designed so that you could spot a Chisum beef a long way of.

Powerful and wealthy, John Chisum ruled his kingdom with an iron hand; even though friendly and gregarious, he was first a businessman. His strong Texas cowboys patrolled his range, and any stragglers or mavericks happening by soon sported a fancy Jingle Bob. Enterprising and farsighted, he knew the potential value of cattle. When the Civil War ended, thousands of unbranded mavericks roamed the range. They belonged to no one and were there for the taking, so he did just that, adding thousands more to his herds.

This practice rubbed many a festering wound raw since the

natives had long considered the cattle as their own free meat supply. Being in such abundance, their value had always been low, so no one before Chisum had cared to round them up and into his corral. His actions, coupled with the fact that the Texan insurgence in itself was not very palatable to the Mexican people, continued to multiply ill feelings.

In 1872 Chisum acquired a huge government contract to supply ten thousand head of cattle to the Indians at Bosque Redondo near Fort Sumner, but his herds were depleted by the maurauding Apache, Mexican and white outlaws who were now stealing back, so he was forced to go to Texas for four thousand head to fulfill the contract.

His enterprise growing by leaps and bounds, he had built South Springs Ranch in 1873, close to the small village of Roswell, and had moved his operations there. It is ironic and hard to believe that this seemingly impregnable dynasty was to be toppled ten years later by a mere signature, his own, carelessly and hastily scribbed on a crumpled piece of paper, and that because of it he would die a broken man. Two shrewd promoters, known as Wilbur and Clark had acquired his signature and proceeded to establish a meat packing firm at Fort Smith, Arkansas, conducting business under the name of Wilbur, Chisum, and Clark. By using his good name, they had sunk him into debt to the tune of $85,000 in promissory notes.

When the fake company disbanded, Chisum being the only solvent member was called upon for payment of the debts and sued in the Texas courts. The court decided in his favor, and the case was settled. After four years, according to Texas law, the statute of limitations took effect and they were declared null and void. In the belief that everything was settled, Chisum moved back to his New Mexico ranch and continued his business as before. In 1875, perhaps expecting more trouble, he quietly sold his interests to Colonel R.D. Hunter of St. Louis, Missouri, but through some arrangement continued to operate the ranch as his own. In the meantime, Willie Rosenthal of Santa Fe had gone to great lengths to collect and purchase the supposedly worthless promissory notes. A series of lawsuits followed, one of them claiming that the transfer of property had been only to prevent his creditors from recovering his indebtedness. It also erroneously listed the transfer date as 1877. Regardless of this, on November 14, 1884 Judge Hamilton entered a decree finding in favor of the plaintiffs and appointing P.L. Vanderveer as special master to sell enough of the Chisum holdings to recover $57,030.86, said amount to be paid to the plaintiffs. A month later John Chisum died in Eureka, Arkansas, and was buried in Paris, Texas, the village he had founded.

When he began his operations in Lincoln County, Chisum had made good friends with a lawyer, Alexander McSween, and John Tunstall, a fellow rancher, having had some business dealings with them. They established a retail store and a bank in opposition to the Murphy, Dolan, and Riley group, who up to then had been the unchallenged political and business leaders of the county. Both competitive stores were located in Placitas, later to be called Lincoln, the county seat. The Murphy group was the same one to whom Jesse Evans and the Seven Rivers Warriors pledged their allegiance and into whose employ they had solicited and enlisted the services and talents of the nefarious Billy the Kid.

Alexander McSween, too, was a fairly new arrival. With his wife of eighteen months he had arrived in Placitas from Eureka, Kansas in March of 1875. Thirty-one years old and already a lawyer, he was searching for a place to settle down and establish his practice, build a home and raise a family. He had graduated from the University of St. Louis in 1869 at the age of twenty-five, and had intentions all along of coming out west. Santa Fe, one hundred and sixty miles north had truly been his intended destination, but something seemed to draw all of these men to Lincoln; perhaps it was the friendliness of the people, or the hand of fate which drew them in. It was to be a fatal mistake, one to be regretted just a little later in his short career, but with the help and able persuasion of Laurence G. Murphy, whom they had just met, they settled in Lincoln town.

They had been camped at Punta de Agua close to Las Vegas when they met up with Miguel Otero, a member of the territorial legislature who was also camped at the green oasis.

It was said that after a friendly visit, Otero had given them a letter of introduction to Major Murphy and outlined the tremendous opportunities available to them in the territory. L.G. Murphy and Company became McSween's first customers even before he had a chance to hang up his shingle and open his doors.

His brilliant and enterprising young wife, the former Susan Hummer of Atchison, Kansas, soon proved to be a real asset to the business. Outgoing and friendly, she fast became an active part in the community. Her new found friends soon took all of their financial and legal matters to her husband, and his business thrived. The major part of his business, however, came from the Murphy-Dolan Company until one day two of Murphy's gunmen were caught rustling cattle from Chisum's herd and driving them into the Murphy corrals.

Chisum had filed numerous complaints against them before, but to no avail. Once the sheriff, a bosom buddy of Murphy's, had arrested them and left the jail door unlocked, or simply closed it with a twist of wire, making it easy for them to kick it open in a few seconds, and after their escape he never attempted a second arrest, permitting them freedom without further hindrance of any kind. This time, however, it was different; they had been caught red-handed, so he had been forced to confine them a bit more forcefully, and had sent a message to Murphy. Murphy, of course, went to his lawyer to prepare their defense and secure their immediate release. His legal and religious upbringing deeply offended, McSween refused, saying that he could not conscientiously defend them knowing that they were both guilty and deserved to hang. Irritated over his refusal, Murphy explicitly ordered him to prepare their defense.

Already up to his gullet with the shadiness of so many of the company's business deals, and relieved to get out from under, McSween tendered his immediate resignation as his personal and business lawyer. Angered, Major Murphy ordered him out, and assured him vindictively that he would someday pay dearly for his disloyalty. Having fully vented his rage on him he stomped into his office, slamming the door; his curse remaining, however, to hang ominously over a stunned McSween.

Laurence G. Murphy had had good beginnings, but his immense power was now obviously going to his head. A Catholic, he had studied for the priesthood, but his worthy plans were changed unfortunately with the advent of the Civil War. He had joined the Army and reaching the rank of Major had come to New Mexico with the U.S. Army's California column. He had been mustered out at Fort Stanton at the end of the war and immediately set up a store at the old fort in partnership with Colonel Emil Fritz who had been discharged at the same time.

Later, Murphy, having sold his interest in the store, pulled up stakes and moved to Lincoln. With Dolan and Riley, he established the company which was to become the most powerful, leading business and political ruling group of the area. Like all other company stores, this one also kept its clientele in continuous peonage and bondage, always indebted to it, and owing it more than a man could possibly ever earn.

Their ranching business was also thriving. Their herd was laughingly called "the miracle herd," because no matter how many beefs went to market, they were always replenished "miraculously," often by the next day. Jesse Evans and his industrious gang kept themselves busy.

This was the only period of time in which it might be said that Billy the Kid worked for Major Murphy. With the others, he brought him all the cattle he could rustle at five dollars a head.

Major Murphy had been known to be rather heavy with the pencil at the store, and this must have been on McSween's mind when a few days after leaving his employ, he wrote:

Laurence G. Murphy and Emil Fritz doing business under the style of L.G. Murphy & Company had a monopoly on the sale of merchandise in this city and used their power to oppress and grind out all they could from the farmers, and to force those who are opposed to them to leave the country. For instance, the farmers would buy merchandise from them at exorbitant prices and were compelled to turn in their produce in payment

at prices to suit L.G. Murphy & Company, and if a
farmer refused to do so, he'd be subjected to intimi-
dation; the whole judicial system is used unwittingly to
accomplish that object. The result was that L.G.
Murphy & Co. were absolute monarchs of Lincoln
County and repressed their subjects with an oppressive
iron heel.

McSween's report was written mainly for his own records,
which he kept in good order, but also to explain on paper his
many reasons for leaving "the company." Shortly after
leaving, however, he started having more than his share of
problems. Murphy's former business partner at Fort Stanton,
Colonel Emil Fritz, had departed for Germany in poor
health. He had written a joyful letter from Stuttgart
regarding his greatly improving health, but in 1874, soon
after its arrival, he passed away.

He left behind a $10,000 insurance policy with his brother
Charles Fritz and his sister Emilie Fritz Scholand as bene-
ficiaries. They, in turn, had retained McSween to collect the
policy which the New York based company was refusing to
pay.

In the spring of 1876 McSween journeyed to New York
City at their request, and hired a New York lawyers firm to
help him pry it lose. The expert New York lawyers finally
met with success, and collected the policy, charging the
estate the absurd sum of $2,851.06. McSween returned to
Lincoln with the balance of the money also billing the estate
the sum of $3,998 for his fees and expenses. Between the
New York lawyers and the McSween firm they had practically wiped out the complete inheritance. Only $3,150 was
left of the Fritz estate.

Time went by, but for some obscure reason, McSween
failed to make payment to the estate. Perhaps he felt there
were other heirs; Fritz's parents were still alive in West
Germany.

It is interesting to note that it was the Murphy company
that was more interested than anyone else in his turning the
money over. What plans did they have to extricate it from
the two heirs? Was Lawyer McSween perhaps trying to keep

the funds from the clutches of the Santa Fe ring? Whatever his reasons for withholding it, it provoked the only instance in which any valid questions were ever raised as to his integrity and honesty. Murphy, claiming that Fritz had owed him money from their previous partnership, charged the lawyer with fraud and obtained one warrant for his arrest and another attaching of his business and personal holdings in Lincoln.

McSween by this time was quite prosperous. The mercantile business which he operated in company with the wealthy young Englishman Tunstall, was thriving. Their bank, in the same building, was also doing quite well. Because of their honesty and fairness with the farmers and ranchers, they now commanded most of Murphy's former trade, and were growing at a steady pace. In contrast, Murphy's business had dropped considerably, and he was now tottering on the brink of bankruptcy.

His anger and animosity knew no bounds. He would find some way to ruin them and get them out of the country, he vowed, if it was the last thing he did. With the help of the U.S. District Attorney, to whom he was deeply indebted and mortgaged, he would bring them to their knees. His wrath and vengeance was not new to Lincoln. The county and the village had seen nothing but trouble since the coming of the gringo.

Lincoln County had been established by the New Mexico Territorial Legislature of 1869, and was the largest county in the United States or its territories. It consisted of what is now Chaves, Lea, Otero, Eddy, De Baca, Lincoln and Roosevelt Counties, an area of over twenty-five thousand square miles. Unfortunately, it had become the dumping grounds for every unsavory character running from the law. They had been pouring in from all areas of the country to the constant chagrin of the peaceful natives. Hated for the simple reason that they could never participate civilly and peaceably in the rich Mexican and Spanish culture and customs, they preferred to disrupt and destroy. Called "Tejanos" by the natives, whatever their origin, the term was disparaging in intent and did not mean simply that they came from Texas. The major characters in what was to be known as the

"Lincoln County War," were all outsiders, some having come from Ireland, others from Germany, England, France, Nova Scotia, Poland, Canada, and just about every state in the union but the New Mexico Territory.

On December 20, 1873, right about midnight, a gay wedding dance in Placitas had been disrupted by a rowdy, ignorant Texas bunch, recent arrivals from Lampassas County, and five villagers had been slain. The five Horrell brothers, Ben, Sam, Martin, Tom and Merritt, together with their brother-in-law Ben Turner and two friends, J.D. Scott and Zacariah Crumpton, had swooped into town, shot out the kerosene lanterns in the dusty dance hall, then started shooting wildly into the crowd, "for the fun of it," they said later.

Killed or wounded in the unnecessary fracas were Isidro Padilla, Dario Balazar, Pilar Candelaria and her husband Jose; Isidro Patron and Apolonio Garcia. Juan Patron, whose father had been one of those killed, gave an eye witness account of the one sided battle to the Santa Fe New Mexican, and his deposition was published on January 9, 1874:

> An assault was committed about midnight on a house, on December 20, 1873, where the people had assembled to attend a wedding dance. The doors were broken open, fire was opened through the windows and doors with guns and pistols. In the firing, four men were killed and two were wounded.

A citizens meeting was held on January 3rd in Placitas with L.G. Murphy presiding. J.J. Dolan was elected secretary and Jose Montano, William Brady, and Murphy were empowered to function legally in place of the missing justice of the peace and probate judge, both of whom had departed when the going got rough. A vigilante group was organized, but was never very effective. In the meantime, the half-crazed, wild bunch officially declared war on the village. They came back for another bout, killing Dave Warner, Constable Martinez and ex-sheriff Jack Gylam, and losing three of their own men. Ben Horrell, leader of the Tejanos, was found dead next the morning down by the river where he had laboriously crawled after being wounded, a finger missing on his left hand. Someone had followed him, watching him stagger and stumble down the hill, and when he had stopped kicking, chopped off his finger to take his ring.

Governor Marsh Giddings who had been in office since 1871 offered a $500 dollar reward for the remaining brothers, including the two illiterate nitwits Crumpton and Scott.

On February 2, 1874 another public meeting was held and this time included the governor, General Gordon Granger, commander of all federal troops in the territory; and many representatives of Placitas, including the new sheriff, Albert Mills, and Juan Patron, the newly elected county clerk.

They asked for federal intervention in the feud; the gang, fearing and expecting this, had called it quits and fled to the Texas border. On their way east, however, another member of the group, a latecomer called Edward "Little" Hart killed and mutilated Joe Haskins, a young pioneer who had settled on the banks of the Rio Hondo, only because he had taken a Mexican wife. A relative followed them, and as they slept at camp close to the village of Roswell, shot from ambush and killed their brother-in-law, Ben Turner in his bedroll, and then quickly fled into the night.

Before reaching Roswell, the bloodthirsty group decided to go back and wipe out as many Mexicans as they could in retaliation for their brother-in-law's death. A few miles away, they found their next victims. Five Mexican traders, their wagons loaded with freight, were camped on the outskirts of the village and preparing to ride into town. The murderous gang descended on them, and in no time annihilated them all and took their loaded wagons. Temporarily satiated, they continued on their way east, stopping off only to steal some horses and mules from two travelers named Beckwith and Wellburn.

Up in arms over the horse and mule thefts, the posse was soon after them and caught up to them south of Roswell. Again catching them in their sleep, they showed them the same mercy they had shown the traders, murdering most of the gang in their blankets. They never knew what hit them.

Two managed to flee the scene, elude the posse and took off for the border, never to be seen in the territory again.

The *Daily New Mexican* of January 27th carried an accurate account of the killings but predicted more troubles ahead:

> A private letter of the 21st which has been shown to us from Placitas, county seat of Lincoln County gives the following concerning the unfortunate war between the Texans and the Mexicans. All here is war and rumors of war. The sheriff left yesterday with sixty men to arrest the Harrolds, and from a courier just returned we learned a fight was going on last night. A general distrust prevails throughout the whole section. Every man met is armed to the teeth. Up and down the Rio Hondo a number of ranches have been deserted, and many fine places could be purchased for a song, their owners and occupants being determined to depart from a place where the reign of peace and order will apparently not be re-established for a long time to come.

The newspaper's predictions were prohetic: the ambience of the county would be lawless, violent and mistrustful for many years to come. Hangings, shootings, duels and outright murder were to be the common order of the day.

One such was the murder of Robert Casey, well-known, respectable rancher who had come to New Mexico in 1867. He was ambushed from behind a garden wall in Placitas by one William Wilson, while attending a political meeting, and soon died of his wounds. It was assumed by some that Wilson had been hired to do the job by Casey's political enemies, while others claimed to have witnessed an earlier argument over either unpaid wages or a loan. Wilson was tried and convicted of murder in the first degree and two months later was executed by hanging. It was the first legal hanging in Lincoln County, and was publicized so well, perhaps to act as a deterrent, that it attracted just about everybody in the territory.

At twelve o'clock noon on a cold December 10th, 1875, amidst a county fair, carnival-type atmosphere, Willie Wilson paid for his crimes—twice, it was said. The hanging was bungled so badly that for years it was known as "the double hanging." The prisoner had arrived on schedule at 11:00 o'clock in the morning escorted by Company G of the U.S. Cavalry, under the command of Captain Stewart Gilmore. After the prisoner had shaken hands with everyone he knew, received his *Santos Oleos* from the priest, his jaw set firmly, he squared his shoulders and climbed the half dozen steps to the gallows. He took a deep breath of God's free gift to living things—fresh air—and waited for the hood that would cover his face, and the hangman who would set his noose. He was ready—as ready as he would ever be. Why didn't they get it over with? he thought. There was a commotion below; Captain Saturninio Baca, acting sheriff, had decided to stay the execution for half an hour. The cruelty of prolonging the preliminaries hit the villagers like a ton of bricks, and they stormed as one towards Baca. Shaken by their angry faces and violent protests, Baca ordered the hangman to proceed with the execution.

Finally, after much ceremony, the trap door dropped out from under his feet and the prisoner writhed in agony at the end of the rope. After ten minutes he was cut down and placed in a wooden coffin for the doctor's pronouncement. After a quick inspection, a surprised Dr. Corballo announced that the prisoner was still alive. He was removed from his coffin, the rope attached to his neck again, the crowd ceremoniously helping to lift his two-hundred pound body back up to the gallows where he was hanged for the second time. This time after twenty minutes he was finally declared dead.

The vigilante group which had previously been ineffective was obviously still in operation, because when Jose Segura from San Patricio was arrested for horse theft, they took the law into their own hands. After his arraignment by J.B. Wilson, justice of the peace, he was being escorted to the Fort Stanton jail for safekeeping when his guards were overpowered and he was taken prisoner by seventeen masked men and shot. His abductors were never apprehended.

Such was the state of affairs in Lincoln town when Billy

came onto the scene. He had had second thoughts. He had been riding with the Seven Rivers Warriors only a short time and had realized that he didn't care for their company one bit. He tangled with Billy Morton often and would have loved to see the skinny, tobacco-chewing Virginian pull his gun.

It was late in the fall of '77 when he made his move. He had met John Tunstall, the wealthy Englishman, and had taken a liking to him immediately, perhaps seeing in him the father or older brother he had never known, even though Tunstall was only twenty-five. Billy, a young seventeen at the time, would be eighteen on November 23rd.

Tunstall offered him a job and Billy accepted it immediately, explaining to him that he was with Evans and helping the other side, but was anxious to make a change. He also had a job to do for John Chisum, he said, but it would take less than two weeks and then he'd be ready to ride.

Billy rode into camp and looked around. He had decided to make a clean breast of his decision right away and right now was about as good a time as any. There was Jesse Evans and George Davis who was said to be his brother, and Billy Morton and Frank Baker, the two that McSween had refused to defend and was now prosecuting. There were also McDavids, Tom Hill and Miquel Segorio. Other warriors were most probably nearby at the time too.

After a bitter argument, Billy, smouldering with rage, rode off into the night. He arrived at Frank Coe's ranch on the Ruidoso to spend the night with his friends, eventually staying on through the months of November and December.

Perhaps two related incidents which had happened two years before may just have been part of the reason that Billy decided to leave the Murphy-Dolan-Riley group. He knew that Riley was deeply hated by the Mexican people, and when he found out why, he knew he was justified in having switched sides. Riley and John Copeland had murdered two young Mexican boys in cold blood who were employed at Copeland's ranch, only because they had attempted to run away. The young boys had told their friends that they had previously been threatened with death merely for answering back to their bosses.

Juan Patron quickly organized a posse to arrest the

assassins Riley and Copeland and bring them to justice, but as they were in the process of arresting them, a large contingent of soldiers from Fort Stanton showed up, halting the arrest and instead arrested several of Patron's posse.

As Patron angrily rode off, cowardly John Riley raised his rifle and shot him in the back. Even though there were over fifty witnesses no charges were over filed against him. This was just another example of the one-sided law under the apostles of the Sante Fe ring.

Patron tottered between life and death for a long time, but eventually regained his health. Even though he was not vengeful, he would live to see the demise of Riley's ill-gotten holdings and of Riley himself.

Chapter Four

Billy Joins Tunstall

Riding to Tunstall's ranch, Billy's thoughts dwelled on the well-educated young Englishman; he didn't really belong in this violent, untamed country, he thought, with his mild manner and soft looks. When they shook hands, he recalled with a smile that Tunstall's hands though strong and firm, were also soft and smooth, like a poet's. Automatically, Billy looked down at his own weather-beaten, rough, calloused hands.

He treated me royally, Billy thought. Even though he could never compare with the well-educated man mentally, he had treated him like an equal, and they had made good conversation together. Billy was a good conversationalist and was well informed on the matters of the day. He could never get hold of a newspaper without going through it thoroughly from the first headline to the last want ad.

Billy hadn't received much of an education during those early years in Silver City and Santa Fe, but he was naturally gifted and had learned much from experience. He possessed his goodly share of that most universally recognized necessary quality, common sense. And while many of his acquaintances went through life illiterate and uneducated, Billy had taught himself. By comparison, he could compose a letter and read quite well.

As he rode to the ranch, Billy had no inkling of what fate had in store; had he known, perhaps he would have changed his course; perhaps not.

Early spring of that year found Billy working for a short period at John Chisum's ranch, taking part in a trail drive to Dodge City, Kansas, under the leadership of Bob Speaks, Chisum's trail boss together with Jim and John Jones, brothers. During this trip, John Jones was killed as he rode up to a ranch house in the outskirts of town chasing after a girl.

On his return from Kansas, Billy and Chisum had a violent argument over his wages. It appears that Chisum had promised to pay him five dollars a head for any of his own cattle rerustled from the thieves and returned to him, but had failed to live up to his agreement. From that day forward, Billy would hold a deep grudge against Chisum, and would never trust or speak well of the man again.

Suddenly angry as he recalled the argument with Baker, Billy viciously kicked at a rock, spitting forcefully into the dust, lightly clutching his ever present companion, his gun at his side. Tugging impatiently on his horses reins he tied them quickly, and expertly to a post and swaggered into the Tunstall yard.

"Ey, Beelee," someone hollered out, "llego el Bilito!" Greeted by name by all the Tunstall help, he raised his hand and waved, yelling back in Spanish to all by name.

One fact that could never be suppressed, even after the war had run its course and peace ensued, was that up to this time, Billy was liked and loved by all who knew him, and respected by his enemies. He was still "El Chivito" to the Spanish and Mexicans and many an Anglo too.

His daring exploits and questionable actions might temporarily erase the endearing nickname from their lips, but their loyal affection would emerge again and again.

No matter how many books would be printed attempting to destroy his character and his memory (many of them by relatives of the legal though not necessarily lawful establishment of the times); no matter how many disparaging statements would be issued by the local newspapers; no

65

matter how much power the Santa Fe ring would exert, the people's love for Billy the Kid, child outlaw, adventurer, and true friend, would remain in their hearts throughout all time, never to be forgotten. El Bilito would be mourned after his death.

Billy's new boss John Tunstall had been born in England with a silver spoon in his mouth. His family had been quite wealthy at one time, but when the family fortune, started to dwindle because of mismanagement, he was sent to America in search of better than average investments for their remaining money.

He had arrived in Lincoln County late in 1876, after having met Alexander McSween at the old Exchange Hotel (La Fonda) in Sante Fe, and had become interested in the possibility of the cattle business as a solid investment with an exceptionally good return. According to McSween, property was cheap in Lincoln and low-priced livestock was easy to come by.

Having been thoroughly convinced, the enterprising young investor started looking at prospective ranch properties and other promising businesses, and shortly thereafter Tunstall and Company was born. Nine months later, in August of 1877, the first shipment of goods for their new store arrived. When they were notified that the goods had arrived in Las Vegas and were being shipped by freight wagon to Lincoln, it became apparent to Dolan and Riley that they were in for stiff competition. Even though Murphy had sold his interest in the store to Riley and Dolan a month before, his was the advice they now sought. They needed to plot their future course.

They would not permit the two outsiders to rob them of their well-established trade and ruin their business, they said. However, they were in for another surprise. Tunstall and Company, with the support of big John Chisum, had other far reaching plans which included the establishment of a bank and a land holding company besides the store and the cattle business. To all appearances, they had intention of eventually taking over all profitable business in the county. All nerves rubbed raw, the Lincoln County War would soon be in full swing.

The stage was just now being set for the tragic drama which would be recounted thousands of times in the years to come, researched and written about by countless authors.

The Billy the Kid story would be retold at campfires, homes and schools, to be changed in each retelling by the more immaginative, purified by each rewriting, fallacy separated from fact. A tragic, unforgettable drama which was to shake the very roots of the Cedros, the mud and rock foundations of the adobes, and the pen and quill of the unimpressed and disinterested author at the capitol in Santa Fe, *Ben Hur*, his goal, blocking out all else. Unknown to each other, the characters were one by one taking their respective places for the stranger-than-fiction drama of frontier life which would soon play to a full house. The smouldering volcano which had for so long been threatening to erupt could no longer hold its fiery force.

The Murphy-Dolan-Riley group, refusing to relinquish their hold, refusing to divest themselves of their great powers, were ready to fight to the finish. The seven rivers warriors, bandits all, ever ready with a gun or a knife, would fight at the drop of a hat; the cause didn't matter as long as it paid well. Jesse Evans, battle lines now drawn between him and the Kid, would stay in to the finish. Frank Baker, hatred flashing in his eyes, would love to shoot Billy even if he were facing the wall. In Santa Fe, the corrupt Santa Fe ring, ruthless and powerful, a finger in every pie, was ready to defend its southeastern New Mexico stronghold at any cost.

McSween and Tunstall, the clean, lily-white business people of principle, but also power-hungry coup d' etat written clearly and indelibly on their faces, were bravely flirting with death. Susan Hummer McSween, brave little vixen of the west, would also play an important role with unequaled courage and feminine determination. Emil Fritz, or rather, his insurance legacy, (he was already a dead man) would also come into play, as would his sister, Emilie Scholand and his brother, Charles Fritz.

A hundred or more other characters would soon come on stage on cue, each to do his part in the tempestuous drama which was to be the focus of attention in the territory for years to come.

The first monkey wrench was thrown into the newly formed Tunstall-McSween Company's gears when on December 7, 1877, Charles Fritz, acting as administrator of his brother's estate, petitioned the courts to order McSween to relinquish the proceeds and remains of the $10,000 insurance policy to him.

His petition read as follows:

I, Charles Fritz, administrator of the estate of Emil Fritz, deceased, respectfully show the court that. A.A. McSween has acted as attorney in said estate, and particularly for the purpose of collecting an insurance policy on the life of said Emil Fritz, deceased, for the sum of $10,000 or thereabouts; that the undersigned is informed and believes that the said A.A. McSween had collected said amount; and he requests the court to make its order directing the said A.A. McSween to deposit or so place said amount of money so that it will be subject to the order of the court and for such further order in said matter as the court may deem expedient for the protection of the estate or to insure it speedy and final settlement.

Three days later Emilie Scholand followed suit and signed her own deposition, further accusing him of embezzlement.

A few days later, Judge Warren H. Bristol issued a warrant for McSween's arrest. It was served on him on December 27, 1877 in Las Vegas, where Mrs. McSween, John Chisum and he were taking a short business trip and vacation. According to Chisum, the group had planned to leave for St. Louis on a buying trip the day after Christmas. T.B. Catron, he said, had telegraphed the sheriff in Las Vegas to find out if they had passed through, and if they hadn't, to detain them when they arrived. They had waited for forty-eight hours, he continued, but when no warrant had arrived they had left in a horse-drawn ambulance.

The group was barely on the outskirts of the village when the sheriff and over thirty rowdy threatening possemen had swooped down on them, dragging them roughly out of the coach, and throwing them to the ground.

"We are not animals or murderers," McSween had said, demanding more humane treatment. They were taken to the jail at the courthouse, while a more courteous member of the posse escorted Mrs. McSween back to the hotel.

After posting bond the next day, John Chisum was released. His good friend, however, was not released until four days later, pending the arrival of the warrant on embezzlement charges. Upon its receipt he was transported back to Mesilla for arraignment.

Every possible charge, trumped up and otherwise was thrown at him. Chisum had four different suits served on him and he was returned to jail when he refused to pay up on a judgement won against him before by Puerto de Luna grocer, Alexander Grezelachowski. The old, supposedly obsolete promissory notes of the "Wilber, Chisum and Clark" fiasco, amost ten years old, also emerged. When all else failed, false charges for resisting arrest were leveled against Chisum, then quietly dropped. In early March he was finally permitted to return home. This was a mere warming up of the guns, the first volleys to be fired on the McSween-Chisum coalition, and which would later include their friend, the wealthy Englishman, Tunstall,

The day after his return from Las Vegas, McSween was slapped with a writ of attachment on all his property and possessions. It was signed by Charles Fritz and Emilie Scholand, with the blessings of J.J. Dolan. Meanwhile a letter written by District Attorney Rynerson had come into McSween's hands. It was written on February 14th in Las Cruces, and was addressed to John Riley and James Dolan. The letter strongly hinted at a high-level legal conspiracy and would be valuable evidence later at the Dudley court of inquiry. The poorly written (for a district attorney) and sparsley punctuated letter follows:

Law office of William L. Rynerson
District Attorney, 3rd Judicial District N.M.
Las Cruces, N.M. February 14, 1878.

Friends Riley and Dolan,

I have just received letter from you mailed 10th inst. Glad to know that you got home OK and the business was going on OK. If Mr. Weidman interfered with or resisted the sheriff in discharge of his duty Brady did right in arresting him and anyone else who does so must receive the same attention. Brady goes into the store in McSween's place and takes his interest. Tunstall will have same right then he had heretofore but he neither must obstruct the sheriff or resist him in his discharge of his duties. If he tries to make trouble the sheriff must meet the occasion firmly and legally. I believe Tunstall is in on the swindles of the rogue McSween. They have the money belonging to the Fritz estate and they must be made to give it up. It must be made hot for them, the hotter the better; this is especially necessary now that it has been discovered that there is no hell. It may be that the villain Green "Juan Bautista" Wilson will play into their hands as Alcaldo. If so he should be moved around a little. Shake that McSween outfit up till it shells out and squares up and then shake it out of Lincoln. I will aid to punish the scoundrels all I can. Get the people with you. Control Juan Patron if possible. You know how to do it. Have good men about to aid Brady and be assured I shall help you all I can for I believe there was never found a more scoundrally set than that outfit.

Yours & C,
W.L. Rynerson

There was little wonder then that with all the proferred backing and support from the legal establishment that the Dolan-Riley group would be spurred on to even greater atrocities.

Controlling Juan Patron itself was easier said than done. Square-jawed and handsome, Patron was the recognized leader of the Mexican people. Honest and well-educated, he was respected by the citizenry as had been his father, the late Isidro Patron. Taken under the wings of Archbishop Lamy in his youth, he had been educated in the Catholic schools of

Santa Fe, and later on received his degree from Notre Dame in Indiana. On his return home he had married Beatriz Labadie, daughter of Lorenzo Labadie, prominent Las Vegas pioneer settler.

After the attempted murder by Riley, when he shot him in the back, it was presumptuous of Rynerson even to suggest that Patron could be controlled. He would side with the McSween faction and Billy the Kid against the ring anytime and would until his death in 1884 be a thorn in their side.

In 1878, at the age of twenty-three he had been elected by his people to the House of Representatives and had served as speaker of the house. The remarkable young leader died at the hands of an assassin, Mitch Maney, in Puerto de Luna, on April 9, 1884. It was suspected, but never thoroughly proven that his death had been an aftermath of his stand during the Lincoln County War.

In Lincoln, Sheriff Brady, having received the district attorney's blessing and the writ of attachment, proceeded to inventory all of the merchandise in the Tunstall-McSween store, the store property, their bank and law offices, and even their homes, land and all their furnishings. In the meantime, Brady's deputy, J.B. Matthews, was authorized to go to Tunstall's ranch and follow suit with his property, the furnishings, and livestock. With Brady's deputizing Matthews, a Dolan employee, it was apparent as to who was calling the shots. Brady, who had up to now been an honest, efficient public servant, was permitting himself to be led and used by the vindictive Dolan, and the backstabber Riley—a weakness which he would soon regret.

On January 18, 1878, John Tunstall wrote a blatantly accusatory letter to the editor of *The Independent* at Mesilla. Written in anger and in retaliation for the many injustices committed by the law against McSween and himself, the letter would prove to be the bombshell that would start the war. Later on, it would be proven correct. His letter started off with an excerpt from the governors' message to the legislature for that year:

> *The present sheriff of Lincoln County has paid nothing during his present term of office.*

71

To the Editor of the Independent:

The above extract is a sad and unanswerable comment on the efficiency of Sheriff Brady and can not be charged upon "croakers." Major Brady, as the records of the county show, collected over twenty-five hundred dollars of Territorial funds. Of this sum Alexander A. McSween, Esq. of this place paid him over fifteen hundred dollars by check on the First National Bank of Santa Fe, August 23, 2877. Said check was presented for payment by John H. Riley, Esq. of the firm of J.J. Dolan and Company. This last amount was paid by the last named gentleman to Underwood and Nash for cattle. Thus passed away over fifteen-hundred dollars belonging to the Territory of New Mexico. With the exception of thirty-nine dollars, all the taxes of Lincoln County were promptly paid when due.

Let not Lincoln County suffer the delinquencies of one, two or three men.

By the exercise of proper vigilance the taxpayer can readily ascertain what has become of what he has paid for the implied protection of the commonwealth. It is not only his privilege but his duty. A delinquent taxpayer is one thing, but a delinquent tax collector is worse.

J.H.T.

Furious J.J. Dolan stormed into the offices of *The Independent* and presented them with his own handwritten response, dated the day after Tunstalls:

Las Cruces, NM. Jan 29, 1878

To the Editor of the Independent
Dear Sir:

In answer to a communication in reference to taxpayers of Lincoln County, published in your issue of the 26th and signed J.H.T., I wish to state that everything contained therein is false.

In reference to Sheriff Brady, I will state that he deposited with our House Territorial funds amounting to nearly $2,000 subject to his order and payable on demand. Owing to sickness in Sheriff Brady's family he was unable to be in Santa Fe in time to settle his account with the terrotory. This I hope will explain satisfactorily why the governor made our county out to delinquent in his message.

If Mr. J.H.T. was recognized as a gentleman and could be admitted into respectable circles in our community, he might be better posted on public affairs. For my part I can't see the object of Mr. J.H.T's letter, unless it is to have the public believe that Alexander A. McSween is one of the biggest taxpayers in the county, when in fact he is one of the smallest.

Sheriff Brady is ready at any time to show uneasy taxpayers what disposition he has made of the money paid by them; he can also show clean receipts from the Territorial treasure for his account.

Respectfully,
J.J. Dolan

In Santa Fe, Catron scurried from the bank to the treasurer's office, in his hand a leather moneybag, enough in it to bail out the tax collector-sheriff of Lincoln County.

McSween's cancelled check eventually made it back into his hands, endorsed by John Riley and Sheriff Brady, payable to the Underwood and Nash Cattle company, a strange discrepancy which could not be so lightly brushed aside, yet which was never prosecuted.

Chapter Five

John Tunstall Dies

It was the eighteenth day of February, 1878, when Jacob B. Matthews, Sheriff Brady's deputy, and his posse arrived at the Tunstall ranch on the banks of the Rio Feliz. An icy wind had been blowing all morning and the banks of the river were completely iced over. Many of the ranchers claimed it was one of the coldest winters they had ever experienced in the area or even in the territory. In Santa Fe, *The Daily News Mexican* of February 2nd had reported that "more snow has fallen in this region during the present winter than had been known for years to our oldest citizens." Regardless of the uncomfortable freezing weather, the posse rode in after Matthews, cursing and yelling at the morning cold, their horses' hooves crunching loudly as they broke through the ice and hard crusted snow at the river crossing.

The unruly posse, hardly amenable to control or restraint was composed of several of the same cattle rustlers and gunmen who had worked for Riley and Dolan. The Seven Rivers Warriors of course were there in full regalia; there was Jesse Evans, their leader, Frank Baker, William Morton, Tom Hill, Andrew L. Roberts (Buckshot), George Hindman, and according to some reports J.J. Dolan himself. It was apparently this same kind of posse that Sheriff Brady had attempted to warn and instruct his deputy about a few days previously.

On February 15th, when Matthews was already on his way to the ranch, Brady had dispatched a messenger with a letter of caution, a letter written probably more to exonerate himself later on should there be an inquiry than for delivery:

Dear Sir:
You must not by any means call on or allow to travel with your posse any persons who are known to be outlaws. Let your Mexicans round up the cattle and protect them with the balance. Be firm and do your duty according to law and I will be responsible for your acts.

I am sir, respectfully yours,
William Brady, Sheriff, Lincoln Company

The letter was forceful and to the point, and although well intended, a little too late. The attachment of the McSween and Tunstall property proceeded in a jubilant, jocular vein. Bob Widenman had been in charge of the store during Tunstall's absence, and had protested vigorously, but to no avail. When he tried to point out to Matthews that the store belonged to Tunstall and not McSween, Matthew just shrugged his shoulders, saying everyone knew McSween had an interest in everything Tunstall did and vice versa. Turning from him, Matthews quickly moved from one area of the building to the other, finally quitting it for the ranch. It was late in the evening, so he postponed his work until the next day.

On his way home from Las Vegas, a weary Tunstall dropped in at Dick Brewer's farm close to San Patricio. He was completely exhausted from the long dusty trip, and hoped to clean up, eat some good grub and relax for the rest of the day, when his foreman hit him with the bad news. At this moment, he said, Matthews men were inventorying the merchandise at his store. His long anticipated return home to his ranch would have to wait until this business was settled.

Arriving at the store, Tunstall was appalled to find all sorts

75

of hangers-on lolling around his usually busy enterprise; the shutters were drawn, and Deputy F.G. Christie was doing a thorough inventory. Outside the store, Tunstall had left two of his employees, whom he had picked up at Brewer's Ranch, armed to the teeth and keeping watch. They were Fred Waite and Billy the Kid. At the corrals behind the store, he had left John Middleton, Bill McCloskey and Godfrey Gauss. With him was his store boss, Widenmann.

After a rough decision he finally permitted them to continue their inventory, instructing Billy and his men to take the six horses and pair of mules from the corrals and lead them to the ranch. Surprisingly, Brady had agreed that they were Tunstall's own private property and should be exempt from the attachment. This was a whim, really, for the wholesale attachment of his store and goods for another man's debt was at best highly improper and illegal.

When Deputy Matthews arrived at the ranch with the writ of attachment, he was met by a copious display of hate-filled stares. Most of the Tunstall men were already there. There were Brewer, Middleton, The Kid, Gauss, Widenmann, Waite, and McCloskey.

Matthews bravely approached the house and stated his purpose. He was here, he said, to attach and confiscate all the McSween and Tunstall herd in the name of the law. He showed his deputy's badge and his attachment orders. Dick Brewer stepped up in front of his men and stated emphatically that he would be permitted to go through the herd and cull out any McSween cattle he could find, but under no circumstances was he driving off any of his boss's herd.

The band of outlaws shifted nervously in their saddles, some of them sounding off with their own opinions as to what should be done, shrugging off the hate-filled eyes glaring at them from the porch. With Matthews was the same coterie of rustlers as before, horse thieves and killers; more like a band of outlaws out on a vendetta than a legal posse serving a writ. Added to Matthews' pack were Manuel Segovia, shifty-eyed killer and mule thief, better known as the Indian; old standby Frank Baker, and John Long.

As they bargained, Dick Brewer, always the diplomat, called to Godfrey Gauss the cook, who was on the porch, to prepare food for all and they would talk out their problems during the meal. Tensions eased.

Matthews, softened by the good food and fair treatment, had agreed just to check the herd, even though his explicit orders were to attach all the cattle, when Robert Widenmann, irked by the presence of Evans and his gang, spoke up. He directed his words to Matthews, asking his permission as a commissioned U.S. Deputy Marshall to arrest Jesse Evans, Hill and Baker. Matthews of course refused, saying that if he should permit it, the ranchers in the party would be made to suffer for it by Dolan.

Widenmann, recalling how all three had serious charges against them, had escaped jail and still were made members of a legal posse, asked Matthews point blank: "Billy, why did you allow those men to come on the posse with you in the first place?"

"I didn't invite them," Matthews pouted; "they came along of their own free will. Jess wanted to find out if you really had a warrant for his arrest," he added.

At this point the Kid was just staying in the background; he was probably wondering what kind of unholy complicated mess he'd gotten himself mixed up in. He was just realizing how deep-rooted and serious the Lincoln County troubles were. What he didn't realize was that before long he would be the main character in the whole bloody murderous affair.

As they continued their supper in the warm, comfortable house, Evans, with a smirk, asked Widenmann, "Do you really want to arrest me?"

"You'll find out soon enough when I do,'. Widenmann retorted. "Go ahead and try it," Evans said, "if you don't mind getting a bullet hole through your thick scalp."

Baker, irritated and itching for a fight, threw back his chair as he stood up. "What the hell's the use in talking," he said. "Let's get the thing going and kill the damned S.O.B.'s."

Finally placated, the posse left amidst grumblings from the more itchy fingered ones, and Tunstall's men retreated back into the house to plot further action. They agreed that Tunstall, still at the store, should be notified of the proceedings. Brewer decided to stay at the ranch in case Matthews should sneak back and try for the cattle, and sent Billy, Waite and

Widenmann instead. Deeply disturbed by the turn of events, Tunstall and the men rode to McSween's house to discuss matters. At one point in their conversation he vowed to McSween that under no circumstances was he going to sacrifice a single man for all the cattle or property in the world.

From there the group went to Chisum's ranch only to find out that John Chisum was still in jail in Las Vegas and his brother Pitzer flatly refused to get involved. "They start everything and are most to benefit, but they don't want to get involved," Billy thought sarcastically.

On the way to the ranch, Tunstall cautioned his men to exercise restraint. No matter what happened, he said, he wanted no bloodshed. Eight miles away at Pauls ranch, Deputy Matthews' posse had rendezvoused. They had been joined by the twenty or so Mexican men Matthews had said would be in charge of driving the cattle while the posse would be the fighting force. Matthews, it appears, had changed his mind about going all the way back to Lincoln to report to Dolan and, spurred on by his gunmen, had agreed to go back and take the cattle by force.

The Tunstall boys were all ready and waiting. They had oiled and readied their arms and cut holes at strategic points through the ranch's thick adobe wall so one could peek out and shoot through. Tunstall, however, vetoed their plans. They would not fight. Any fighting, he said should and would be done legally in the courts. He still had confidence in the legal system of the county and the New Mexico territory; his men felt otherwise. Bill McCloskey was ordered to leave for Paul's ranch early next morning about three a.m. to advise Matthews of his decision. Tunstall and group would withdraw to Lincoln leaving only Gauss, and "Dutch" Martin Mertz to oversee the counting of the cattle, together with Matthews' representative, and then stay on and care for them until the matter was settled in the courts. Matthews had been ready to accept his fair and logical solution when J.J. Dolan, thirsting for blood, took over. They would go to the ranch and playing it by ear, he said, would decide on the best course when they got there. To him, the best course was one that would degrade and ruin his enemy the quickest. He was not by any means seeking legal solutions; his aim was to cripple and destroy his adversary.

It was late afternoon, February the eighteenth, 1878, when they arrived at the ranch. Mertz and Gauss were the only ones there. As Dolan and Matthews were trying to decide what to do with the cattle, Jesse Evans asked Mertz what had happened to the horses. Tunstall and his group had taken them with them, early that morning, Mertz told him since Sheriff Brady had exempted them from the attachments. Jesse Evans exploded: "Damn it, let's go after them; they took the horses we loaned to Billy the Kid."

It is doubtful that this was true, since Billy and he had been on the outs for quite some time, and the loan had never been mentioned before. It was more likely that it afforded him a good excuse to go out after them. Eagerly, Dolan piped up, "Let's get some of the men after them. If they are overtaken before they reach the plaza we will bring them back here." Buck Morton, the foreman of Dolan's cow camp on the Pecos was placed in charge of the pursuers.

Pantaleon Gallegos had been taking down all of the proceedings for the official records, and when he started to write down Evans", Hills' and Morton's names he was stopped by Dolan, who told him not to. Obviously, he was afraid of the public criticism of his use of known outlaws on a supposedly legal sheriff's posse. Jesse Evans, however, would not be suppressed. "Damn right wer'e going," he said. The posse left, led by a wanted man. The other outlaws were right behind him.

Because of the herd of horses they were driving with Fred Waite driving the wagon, the Tunstall group was making little progress. The day was cold and windy as they neared the Pajarito Mountains. The frozen range loomed monumentally before their eyes as they reached the crossroads of the main way to the hamlet of Roswell and Lincoln, about twenty-eight miles from the ranch they had left that morning.

It was decided that Waite would stick to the road to make better time, while the rest of the men would take to the trails on the west side of the Pajaritos and from there strike out north to Lincoln. Having left the wagon, they were about ten miles west of San Patricio and four miles from the Rio

Ruidoso when they startled a flock of wild turkeys. Dick Brewer, Tunstall and Widenmann were up ahead, the horses following leisurely in single file through the narrow trail, while Billy and John Middleton were riding rear. Leaving Tunstall alone, Brewer and Widenmann took off in pursuit of the turkeys.

As they rode the crest of the hill, they heard the thundering hooves of a large herd of horses coming towards them from the south. Obscured by pine trees, they were about to alight to investigate when they were met by a hail of bullets from the marauding band. They were taking off for the shelter of the boulders at the base of the hill where they could make a good stand, when they saw the rest of the pack coming up over the hill. They also saw Billy and Middleton as they took to the boulder-strewn hill, and Tunstall, unawares and preoccupied, riding on up ahead. They called to him to take cover, but either he didn't hear them or had no intention of running; he paid them no heed.

The front riders had shifted alone. Tunstall saw them and turned around. As he rode slowly towards them, two shots rang out. Brewer and his party didn't see the killing; they had been scampering through the rocky Chamiso hills and were out of view, but upon discovery it looked like an outright murder.

Sheriff Brady's report to District Attorney Rynerson a few days later attempted to alter the facts when he wrote in part: "And while a portion of the posse was in pursuit of the party, J.H. Tunstall fired on the posse and in the return fire was shot and killed."

Aghast at the murder, many of the posse members quit then and there, refusing to go any further, probably saving Brewer and his men on the hill from complete annihilation. The posse then rode back to Tunstall's ranch to report his death to Deputy Matthews and Dolan. They stated that Tunstall had resisted their arrest, shot at them, and had died in the return fire. From those who had quit the posse would come the true story later, even as they returned to their homes. Completely different from those on the official records, the facts would become common knowledge. Meanwhile, Billy, Brewer, and the others had taken off cross country towards Lincoln on foot, reaching the Placita del Rio Bonito about eleven p.m., and soon the whole village was swarming around them, listening to their sordid story.

By midnight, hundreds of angry people were out in little groups throughout the village; over sixty of them converged on the McSween home to offer their support, but also to listen to the official details of the killing. Their sense of decency and justice outraged, they knew that the law as they had known and accepted it had become more lawless and brutal than the outlaws it was supposed to track. They realized that there was no way they could be expected to arrest and bring to justice from among their own midst those responsible for John Tunstall's murder.

From among his visitors, McSween, now thrust into a position of leadership, requested a volunteer to go to John Newcomb's ranch on the Ruidoso and ask him to bring the body in. Newcomb and his neighbors, Lazaro Gallegos, Roman Paragon, Patrocinio Trujillo and Florencio Gonzales, were up at daybreak next morning and on their way.

They found Tunstall about a hundred yards from where he had been killed, a bullet hole in his chest and another in the back of the head. It was obvious that he had been shot a second time after he dropped on the trail. Their jaws set, minds bent on revenge, an angrier group of men than those who rode in that night with Tunstall's body had never been seen before. "Vengeance is the Lord's," someone quoted from scripture, only to be met by muderous glares. It was too late for preaching, too late for words.

John B. "Squire" Wilson, the justice of the peace, also at McSween's, was directed to prepare arrest warrants for the killers. They were named by Billy the Kid, Dick Brewer, and Middleton as having been Jesse Evans, William Morton, Tom Hill, Frank Baker, George Hindman, and James J. Dolan himself.

Billy, who had been affected deeply by the death, was heard to say that he would never rest until he got everyone of the "low down bastards" who had been on the sheriff's posse. The friendship between Tunstall and him had grown fast, perhaps born of loneliness or a need to belong. Tunstall was thousands of miles away from his family, and Billy, filled with wanderlust, had never had a place to hang his hat, had never really had a place he could call home.

A conflict arose immediately during the inquest between the two physicians called in to perform the autopsy and embalming. Dr. D.M. Appel from Fort Stanton, who had been hired by Sheriff Brady for the unheard of fee of $100, came through with a mild report stating that aside from two bullet holes there were no other bruises on the body. Dr. Taylor Ealy a newcomer who had just arrived in Lincoln from Pennsylvania, stated in his report to the contrary, that in addition to the bullet holes, Tunstall's head had been badly disfigured and his skull had been bashed in after death, probably with the butt of a rifle.

McSween then attempted to serve the warrants. He sent the arresting party in the persons of Constable Atanacio Martinez, and Billy the Kid and Fred Waite for backup support. When the three men arrived at Dolan's store where the outlaw posse was headquartered, Martinez stated his intentions and attempted to enter. Sheriff Brady immediately jumped to their defense, refusing to let him in to serve the warrants, stating that since they had been legally sworn in to serve on the posse, they were immune to arrest. However, he added smugly, since he was sheriff and held the power, he was instead placing *them* under arrest.

Suprised by the turnabout, and since there were fourteen rifles pointing at them, Martinez, Billy and Waite quietly surrendered. They were thrown into jail, where Billy and Waite were to remain for two days. Martinez was released that same afternoon.

Embittered because he had not been allowed to attend his friend's funeral, Billy subconsciously added Brady to his little black list. Tunstall was buried on February 22nd, 1878, a short distance east of his store, in a patch of green grass by the Rio Bonito. A large group of heavily armed friends and McSween sympathizers attended the funeral. It was evident that they were not to be caught without their arms again even at a funeral; Such would be the prevailing atmosphere in the region for years to come.

The day after the funeral, Billy and Waite were released

from jail. It was a Saturday, and even though it was a cold day, there were many more people in the streets than usual. Carriages full of angry settlers and the curious continued to arrive throughout the day.

Billy walked down to the frozen banks of the river. As if in reverence to the mournful mood of the young man and his friend's grave nearby, it was hushed, and silent. Billy poked at the fresh-turned mound of soil, and the still green grasses around it. From wealth and opulence, Tunstall had come from across the sea to give his life for a cause in the Lincoln Territory of New Mexico, and had come to rest on the banks of the Rio Bonito, a beautiful place. May he rest in peace, Billy prayed.

There was a buzzing of excitement and expectancy in the air as Billy walked up the street. In oblivious defiance to the cold wintry air, people strolled through town, shopping or pretending to shop at the few meager stores open.

Nothing unanticipated happened throughout the day, but about five p.m. that afternoon the first of a series of small irritating incidents occured. Robert Widenmann instigated the first one. Still sporting his U.S. deputy marshall's badge, he went to Fort Stanton to see Captain Purrington who was now in charge, requesting back-up support in serving the warrants which he held against Baker, Hill, Evans and Davis for the theft of government mules. Probably appalled and shocked by the senseless murder of Tunstall, Captain Purrington quite readily and unexpectedly agreed.

It was close to dark when Lieutenant Goodwin arrived with a small detachment of soldiers, turning them over to Widenmann. His strategy all laid out, Widenmann led them to Dolan's store, posting them in strategic locations around the building. Then with Martinez, Billy, Waite, Edwards and Middleton he marched into the empty store. They searched it thoroughly but were unable to find the wanted men. They marched on to Tunstall's looted store and arrested the five guards who had been appointed by Dolan. Jim Longwell, James Clark, John Long, Charles A. Martin and George Peppin were arrested without incident and taken to jail.

Having taken over the store legally, Widenmann placed some of his posse in charge, and late at night returned to the fort and discharged the troopers. This would be the only time that the military ever helped the dissident faction led by Alexander McSween. Good assistance it had been too, for it gave them control of the store for a long time.

At the fort, Widenmann bravely suggested the arrest of Sheriff Brady to Lieutenant Goodwin. He claimed that there was, after all, sufficient cause; first of all he had permitted the unlawful, disgraceful posse to operate with his sanction, and secondly he had refused to arrest the known killers of Tunstall. His feelings mirrored those of the majority of the people but still his request would simply be brushed aside.

On the 24th, a group of McSween's friends stealthily made their way through the cold night. They were to rendezvous at his house. Finding him in his bed alseep, they continued to knock until he awoke. They were there to warn him of impending danger to himself and his family if he didn't leave the village at once, they said. His enemies were letting it be known that he was next on their unholy list. Though at first he refused, next day, Monday morning, found him deep in thought, seriously and apprehensively putting his papers in order and preparing a will; leaving all of his goods and possessions to his wife, and naming John Chisum executor, and his wife alternate if Chisum should refuse or for that matter be unable to serve.

On the 27th, in the company of his body guard Deputy Sheriff Barrier from San Miguel County, McSween secretly fled the embattled village. They took to the scrub and Chamiso hills in the upper Pecos River Valley, about twenty-five miles from Lincoln. With plenty of supplies, they camped midway up the high peaks east of the river where they could scan the plains for miles to the west towards Lincoln. About ten miles away, lay the Bosque Grande Ranch, John Chisum's pride and joy. They kept in secret contact with the ranch, which gave them moral support and occasional comfort, replenishing their supplies whenever necessary and from it keeping abreast of the continuing unrest and instability in the county.

Regretting having ever gotten himself involved with such unscrupulous characters as his former clients, McSween started to write a long narrative of the Lincoln County troubles as he saw them. With plenty of time on his hands, he would be able to add many more episodes to it before his death.

In town, two affidavits signed by different members of the posse were causing quite a bit of excitement. They shed some light on Tunstall's murder and verified the many suspicions prevalent in the public mind. Samuel R. Perry's testimony would point an accusing finger at three of the four suspected men as having actually pulled the trigger which resulted in his death:

We arrived at the Felix (Rio Feliz) on the morning of the eighteenth about eight a.m. There we found Martin Mertz who was in charge of the cattle—he was either there or came before we left (I am not positive)—and a cook named Gauss. We inquired about the horses and they told us they had gone but did not know where they had gone. They had left about daylight and thought they had gone to Lincoln but were not sure

Matthews then gave the attachment papers to Morton and told him to take some men and attach the horses. Morton selected Robert W. Beckwith, Wallace Ollinger, Sam Perry, Charles Kruling, Thomas Cockrane, Thomas Green, P. Gallegos, John Hurley, Charles Marshal, Manuel Sagolia, George Kit, Ramon Montoya, George Hindman, Frank Baker, Jesse Evans, and Thomas Hill. The latter three were not called upon, but volunteered, stating that they had a horse from among the horses Tunstall had taken away and that they wished to go after it. I do not remember whether there was any objection made by anyone to their accompanying us, except that Dolan said to either Matthews or Morton that they had better not go. Either Baker, Evans, or Hill replied that a person had a right to go after their property, or something to that effect. I am positive that Dolan did not go with us and Morton and we started after the horses. Hindman, Marshall and myself, having tired horses, brought up the rear.

We had gone about thirty miles when Manuel Sagolia appeared in front of us beckoning us to come on. We trotted on and when we were about half a mile on from our party which was ahead and had overtaken Tunstall's property and party Hindman said, "I heard a shot."

I replied, "I don't think so, a horse stumbled."

"I hear another," he said, and when we reached the top of the hill we saw the horses rounded up and some of our party around them. Morton came up and said Tunstall was killed. I said that it could not be for I did not believe Tunstall was there. He said that he had followed after Tunstall whereupon Tunstall turned and came riding up to him. He had commenced to read the warrant to him, whereupon Tunstall drew his pistol and fired two shots at him. Before Tunstall had fired Jesse Evans called to him to throw up his hands and he would not be hurt. Tunstall disregarded this and fired as above set forth, whereupon he, Jesse Evans and Hill, fired at him and the result of the firing was that Tunstall and his horse were killed.

After the above statement had been made to me, Evans and most of our party being present, I went to the place where Tunstall was lying. I found him on his face, his horse close besides him, their heads being in the same direction. The horse was nearly dead. To put the horse out of its misery, Tom Hill shot it with his carbine. I took his blankets, and Tom Green, Wallace Ollinger, Charles Kruling, George Hindmann and I laid him out by the side of his horse. We did not see his hat, nor did anyone place it under the horse's head. Tom Hill had Tunstall's revolver which he had found eight or ten feet from where the horse had fallen. Tom Hill handed it to Montoya and Montoya handed it to me, and I placed it by Tunstall. I did not examine the pistol. Tunstall's face was bruised by the fall, but it was not mutilated by any of our party. We therefore returned to the Felix with the horses.

We found Dolan by the camp about 500 yards from Tunstall's house. I am positive that Dolan was not with our party that had gone after Tunstall's property after we returned to the Felix. I heard either Baker, Evans, or Hill say the death of Tunstall was a small loss, that he ought to have been killed, or something to that effect. I cannot say which one of the three said this, but one of the three said that Tunstall had tried to have them killed while they were in jail in Lincoln. Except as above set forth, I heard no threats against Tunstall either directly or indirectly. I believe that under the circumstances Tunstall met his death while resisting a legal process. Frank Baker was with Rivers when he brought the papers deputizing Morton and me when the other persons on the Pecos were summoned. Dolan told Morton we were starting after Tunstall's property, to be very careful and to do nothing but what was according to law. While I was laying out Tunstall I heard two or three shots. I am not positive. I inquired what they were shooting about and they said they were shooting at a tree. There was some talk at this time that either Hill or Morton or Evans had shot off Tunstall's pistol. I thought it a little strange that they were shooting at a mark. I do not know who was shooting. I did not think that it was the appropriate time to be doing this. I was busy laying Tunstall out.

The other statement was made by Pantaleon Gallegos who was also on the posse. He testified that he had not been an eyewitness to the shooting, but had been nearby and had heard Bill Morton render an account immediately thereafter. His affidavit closely followed Samuel Perry's and Widenmann's, but in his, Gallegos conspicuously failed to make any mention of Evans and his gang.

Later on Godfrey Gauss would state under oath that it was Matthews who had ordered Pantaleon Gallegos, who was keeping the records, to delete the names of Evans, Hill, Baker and Davis. He also stated that he had heard no one object to their presence and was under the impression that they had been hand-picked for the job by none other than J.J. Dolan. While serving mainly to confuse the public the conflicting stories evidently failed to erase one cold clear fact: Tunstall had been murdered in cold blood, perhaps premeditated; shot point blank by Evans or Morton or both, and finished off by the murderous bloodthirsty mad dog, Tom Hill.

While Dolan disavowed any previous knowledge of the group's plans, rumors persisted that he had let it be known that he would pay a thousand dollars to the man who would kill Tunstall. Upon hearing this, McSween wrote a lengthy letter to Tunstall's father in England, telling him about it and adding that his own head was on the chopping block.

Whether Evans, Baker, Hill and Morton ever collected the blood money was never known, but it remains quite possible that they may all have shared in the reward. Billy, who had never been known to make idle threats, had sworn to get his friend's killers, and the gravity of his threat would very soon be known. The aftermath of the Tunstall murder would bring many repercussions in its wake.

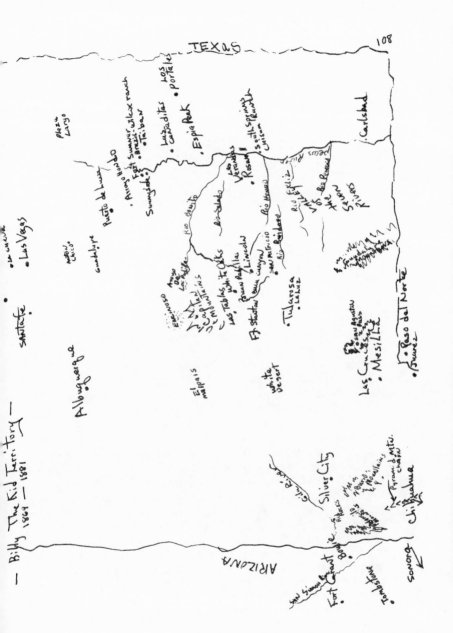

— Billy The Kid Territory —
1864 — 1881

Chapter Six

Vengeance Is The Lord's

The little ranch was a beehive of activity. Dick Brewer, the owner, had summoned his friends, neighbors and fellow workers, and they in turn had summoned their friends. Everyone who had any interest in law and order for their county and who believed in their cause were there. It was agreed by all that a regulatory group was badly needed in the county to keep the law in check; one which would act when the law failed.

After frenzied and sometimes angry discussion, an organization, to be known as "The Regulators," was formed. It would be headed by Brewer himself since he had been Tunstall's ranch boss before his death. It was organized, they said, in the interests of peace, justice, and law and order, with the main objective of bringing to justice the men who had so cold-bloodedly carried out Tunstall's execution.

They promised always to uphold the law, and not take justice into their own hands, but merely to assure themselves and the people that the killers would go to trial at the next scheduled session of court in early April. They felt that there had been such a serious breakdown in the effectiveness of government in the county that the elected officials could no longer impartially enforce the law of the land, and had instead become the willing tools of the notorious Santa Fe ring and its Lincoln County associates.

Dick Brewer, the leader, was a rancher and farmer, working a small spread on the Rio Ruidoso, at the same time having been employed by Tunstall to run his ranch. He was very well liked by everyone, and known as an industrious, sober, non-drinking, non-smoking young man of obviously very few faults. He was born in Vermont in 1851 and had come out west at the age of twenty-one to make a life for himself. He had married a local girl and soon settled down in his little ranch by the river. Jaws set stubbornly, the tousle-haired, green-eyed, rugged young pioneer made plans for the Regulators' first act.

Since they knew that at least some of the former posse members would probably be found at the Dolan cow camp by the Pecos, they decided to attack it en masse. On the morning of March the third, they got their gear together and headed for the river. When they arrived at the camp they found signs that it had been hastily deserted. Someone, probably of their own party, had let the former posse know of the impending raid.

Failing to find anyone there they scouted the vicinity for the next two days, and as they were about to give up and go home, they met up with a group of horsemen riding towards the camp. Recognizing two of the group as the notorious Frank Baker and "Bucks" Morton, they took off in hot pursuit. They had been front riders together with Evans and Hill in the Tunstall ambush. After a five-mile chase with their horses completely tired out and ready to collapse from exhaustion, the two men were easily caught in a dry arroyo bed. Three others, whom Brewer had been unable to recognize, were not followed and permitted to go their way as they raced across the plains.

Immediately forgetting his pledge to uphold law and order, Billy the Kid wanted to kill the two on the spot. "Let's kill the sons a bitches right now," Billy had said. "They didn't give John any mercy either."

He had to be "restrained with the greatest difficulty by others of the party," Morton would write in a letter to his cousin in Virginia later that day.

It was late afternoon when the Regulators arrived at John Chisum's cow camp on the Pecos, and they slept there that night. Next morning they continued their trek downriver to Chisum's ranch where again they arrived too late to go any further and stayed the night.

Some time after supper, Billy Morton, perhaps entertaining a premonition of his impending fate, asked Brewer for permission to write the aforementioned letter to his relative in Richmond, Virginia. Seeing no harm in it, the kindhearted Brewer acquiesced. The letter follows:

South Springs River, N.M.
March 8, 1878

H.H. Marshall
Richmond, Va.

Dear Sir:

It has been some time since I was called upon to assist in serving a writ of attachment on some property wherein resistance had been made against the law.

The parties had started off with some horses which should be attached, and I as deputy sheriff with a posse of twelve men was sent in pursuit of same. We overtook them, and while attempting to serve the writ our party was fired on by one J.H. Tunstall, the balance of the party having been run off. The fire was returned and Tunstall was killed. This happened on the eighteenth of February.

On the sixth of March I was arrested by a constable's party and accused of the murder of Tunstall. Nearly all of the sheriff's party fired at him, and it is impossible for anyone to say who killed him. When the party which came to arrest me and one man who was with me first saw us about a hundred yards distant, we started in another direction when the eleven men fired nearly one hundred shots at us. We ran about five miles until both of our horses fell and we made a stand. When they got to us, they told us if we would give up they would not harm us.

After talking a while, we relinquished our arms and were made prisoners. There was among them one man in the party who wanted to kill me after I had surrendered, and was restrained with the greatest difficulty by others of the party. The constable himself said he was sorry we gave up as he had not wished to take us alive.

We arrived here last night enroute to Lincoln. I have heard that we are not to be taken alive to that place. I am not at all afraid of their killing me, but if they should do so I wish that the matter be investigated, and the parties dealt with according to law. If you do not hear from me four days after receipt of this, I would like you to make inquiries of the affair.

The names of the parties who have arrested me are: R.M. Brewer, J.G. Scurlock, Chas. Bowdre, Wm. Bonney, Henry Brown, Frank McNab, "Wayt" Sam Smith, Jim French and two others, named McCloskey and Middleton, who are friends. There are two parties in arms, and violence is expected. The military is at the scene of disorder and trying to keep peace.

I will arrive at Lincoln the night of the tenth and will write you immediately if I get through safe. Have been in the employ of Jas. J. Dolan and Co. of Lincoln for eighteen months since the 9th of March '77 and have been getting $60 per month. Have about $600 due me from them and some horses, etc. at their cattle camps.

I hope that if it becomes necessary that you will look into this affair, if anything should happen I refer you to T.B. Catron, U.S. Attorney of Santa Fe, N.M., and Col. Rynerson, District Attorney, La Mesilla, N.M. They both know all about the affair, as the writ off the attachment was issued by Judge Warren Bristol of La Mesilla, N.M. and everything was legal. If I am taken safely to Lincoln, I will have no trouble, but will let you know.

If it should be as I suspect, please communicate with my brother Quin Morton, of Lewisburg, West Virginia. Hoping that you will attend to this affair if it becomes necessary and excuse me for troubling you if it does not.

I remain
yours respectfully,
W.S. Morton

Lincoln
Lincoln Co. N.M.

For reasons known to him alone, Morton's friend William McCloskey had arrived at the ranch that evening, pretending sympathy for the McSween side. However, the men had not so easily forgotten that he had been a member of the original Matthews posse (even though not on the one that had killed Tunstall) and was also a friend of both Baker and Morton.

What was he doing here now, presuming to be on their side, they wondered? Was he perhaps a self-appointed protector of his good friend Billy Morton, or was he spying on them, only to relate their every move to Matthews and Dolan later on? Whatever his reasons for being there, he was nevertheless treading on thin ice, risking life and limb among these angry, trigger-happy desperadoes.

Fred Waite and Billy the Kid had been whispering quietly to each other, their angry stares riveted on Baker and Morton, but especially on Morton. He had sensed their animosity and had known their intentions even as he wrote; then after McCloskey's arrival their attention had turned to him.

In Sante Fe, Governor Axtel had decided to visit the front. He had done everything to ensure his own safety, and well being except encase himself in armor before he left that day. At the same moment that Morton sat and wrote his lengthy letter at South Springs Ranch, the governor, after having arrived at Fort Stanton, was preparing to retire for the night. Having arrived rather late in the evening and completely tired out after the long dusty trip, he had bathed and decided to retire early. Next day, they would leave for Lincoln.

The unseasonally warm day found him in the company of J.J. Dolan conducting a rather one-sided investigation. He spoke to no one other than Dolan and his cronies, thereby receiving a rather slanted opinion of the matters involved on which to base his decisions. After three hours in Lincoln, all of them spent with Dolan, he became an instant expert on the troubles of the county and ordered published a proclamation addressed to its citizens. That his actions were intentional and his decision predetermined was soon apparent to all. His stunning proclamation which served only to anger the people and further stir the hornets' nest, read as follows:

LINCOLN COUNTY TROUBLES—
PROCLAMATION BY THE GOVERNOR

To the Citizens of Lincoln County:
The disturbed condition of affairs at the county seat brings me to Lincoln County at this time. My only object is to assist good citizens to uphold the laws and keep the peace. To enable all to act intelligently, it is important that the following facts should be clearly understood:

First—John B. Wilson's appointment by the county commissioners as a justice of the peace was illegal and void, and all processes issued by him were void, and said Wilson has no authority whatever to act as a justice of the peace.

Second—The appointment of Robert Widenmann as U.S. Marshal has been revoked, and said Widenmann is not now a peace officer nor has he any power or authority to act as such.

Third—The president of the United States upon an application made by me as governor of New Mexico had directed the post commander Col. Geo. A. Purrington to assist territorial civil officers in maintaining order and enforcing legal process. It follows from the above statements of facts that there is no legal process in this case to be enforced, except the writs and processes issued out of the third judicial district court by Judge

Bristol, and there are no territorial officers here to enforce these except Sheriff Brady and his deputies.

Now, therefore in consideration of the premises, I do hereby command all persons to immediately disarm and return to their homes and usual occupations under penalty of being arrested and confined in jail as disturbers of the public peace.

S.B. Axtel
Governor

Lincoln, N.M. March 9, 1878

The governor's proclamation was a blow to the Regulators. He had taken sides, completely stripping them of any vestige of legality. On choosing the side of the outlaws, he was thereby condoning the murder of John Tunstall, to wit, official sanction and acceptance of the actions of the outlaw sheriff's posse. While the Dolan supporters were elated, the people as a whole were incensed and seething. At McSween's house a heavy pall of gloom hung suffocatingly in the air. Dick Brewer had arrived with astonishing news that would further entangle the situation, add fuel to the fire and light the fuse that would erupt into the Lincoln County war: Frank Baker, William Morton, and Bill McCloskey had been slain by the Regulators. The atrocity had occurred near the Aguas Negras Spring about five miles from the base of the Captains, he said.

The first report had it that while at the Chisum ranch, Morton had expressed the fear to McCloskey that they would never reach Lincoln alive, and would instead be killed by their captors on the way, at which point, the report said, McCloskey had retorted, "If anybody tries to kill you, they'll have to kill me first." This statement, heard by their guards, added to their suspicions and mistrust.

They had just left the pass at the Aguas Negras Canyon, when Frank McNab rode up front where McCloskey was riding, slightly behind the other two prisoners, and addressed himself directly to him: "I understand that you're the son of

96

a bitch we have to kill first before we can kill the other two." No sooner had McCloskey turned around to answer him, than McNab, pistol in hand, pulled the trigger, sending a bullet through his gut. McCloskey clutched his belly, doubled over with pain and dropped from his horse. He had been taken at his word.

Morton and Baker realizing what had happened, spurred their horses on, making a feeble, desperate attempt at freedom. In one split second, Billy the Kid drew his gun, and with customary lightning speed, put two bullets through their backs. Morton and Baker died instantly and McCloskey, after gasping out a few words, died several minutes later, down in the draw. One discrepancy in this story was that Morton was reported to have nine bullet holes, all through his back. Either there were three premeditated murders in retaliation for Tunstall's death, or as they said, it was an escape attempt. *Quien sabe?*

The report given to Dick Brewer when he rode up (he had been riding tail) was that Morton had grabbed McCloskey's gun and killed him, and that it was only then that they had been forced to shoot them both as they attempted to escape. Whatever really transpired at Dead Man's Draw, as the place later came to be known, remains a secret for all eternity, only to be wondered about and imagined, for no one really knows.

That night Dick Brewer attempted to explain what had happened to a weary, burdened McSween, who sat with his Bible on his knee. He had not wanted violence, and now the three deaths weighed heavily on his mind. He advised Brewer to make his report as constable and then to flee for the hills as he himself intended to do. There would be no holding back the Dolan forces now, he said, especially since they had just received the governor's unqualified blessing, while they themselves were the renegades.

Again with his guard, Deputy Barrier, McSween fled his home. He headed for the sanctuary of the Chisum ranch again, while Brewer returned to his farm and the Tunstall ranch. The Regulators had left immediately after the killings, also towards the Tunstall ranch oblivious to the governor's message of that morning.

On March thirteenth, Tom Hill, who had so viciously

vented his rage on Tunstall's dead body only a month before, also met his fate. During a lull in the county battles, Evans and he had sneaked into a sheep camp by the Tularosa, and finding it empty had started to loot the camp. They had been caught in the act by the camp boss, John Wagner who had been squatting behind a Chamiso bush nearby, answering the call of nature when they arrived. He picked up Hill's rifle, and when they refused to leave, the sprightly old German immigrant shot them full of lead. Hill died instantly, but Evans managed to escape with a minor wrist wound and a bullet through his lungs. Healthy and robust, he healed fast, and in no time was back again with the Dolan flock.

The vendetta continued in full swing; the next series of killings happened in Lincoln on April Fool's Day, 1878. A session of the district court had been scheduled for April the eighth, but had been erroneously posted for April first. Since early morning, wagons had been pouring into Lincoln town, full of bored homesteaders and their families. Any session of the district court was bound to bring plenty of entertainment and excitement. Among the curious were those summoned to Lincoln either as witnesses or as defendants. Sheriff Brady, of course, was there, as was Undersheriff Matthews and many of the deputies who had participated in the Tunstall murder posse. At Tunstall's old store were a good bunch of the Regulators, who had arrived the night before in the evening dark. Since they had all been in separate parts of the county after the three killings in early March, they had a lot to talk about. What irritated many of them the most was that they had to remain in hiding and were sought as criminals, while the other side, as much or more criminal than they, moved about in complete freedom with the authority to arrest or kill them on sight.

All of them—Brady, Murphy, Dolan, the governor, the district judge; Rynerson, the district attorney, his staff, and even Colonel Purrington from Fort Stanton, were a part of that damned "Ruedita" from Santa Fe, they surmised. They weren't very far from the truth. "That ring has ruled long enough," someone said.

"We can't be treated in this manner," another added angrily.

"Here we are, holed up since late last night while they are free to strut up and down the streets like they owned the place."

"Look, there they come now, the dirty dogs," said another. Looking up the road to the right of the store, they saw a group of men coming out of Dolan's store. Past the old Wortley Hotel they trudged, past the McSween residence, their hideout, and by Tunstall's store next door. Led by Sheriff Brady and James Dolan, were Matthews, George W. Peppin, John Long and George Hindmann.

"Let's get 'em now," a hothead hollered, pulling out his revolver only to be stopped by the others and calmed down. Brady and his men walked by without incident, oblivious to the close call they had just had.

On past the Huff home and the old Torreon and into the courthouse grounds they went, where Brady stopped to talk to some people who were lolling outside, chatting with friends. He summoned some men who were leaning against the courthouse walls and others sitting on the steps, prospective members of the jury, and notified them of the error made in posting the scheduled date for court. Court wouldn't meet until April eighth, he advised them.

After delivering his message, they turned around and started back for Dolan's store. As they approached the Tunstall corrals several shots rang out, across the street from Captain Saturninio Baca's house by the old Torreon. Brady in front, fell instantly in the street, while his Deputy Hindmann staggered around a few seconds before he also fell. The rest of the group scattered and took cover. As he lay in the street, Hindmann moaned loudly for water. Of all his associates who had taken cover, not one of them dared to answer his dying plea. Ike Stockton, who was peering out of his saloon next door in the Montano building, heard him, and bravely defying the bullets, ran out with a dipper full and held it to his lips. No one shot in his direction. A few minutes later, Hindmann gasped loudly and died.

Billy heedlessly jumped the adobe fence where they had been lying in wait and ran to the sheriff's body where it lay in the dust. His intention, he said later, was to reclaim his .44 Winchester rifle which the sheriff had confiscated on a

99

previous occasion, and had been sporting at his side. As he stooped down to pick it up a shot rang out from the Cisneros house nearby where Matthews and Long had taken refuge. Blood spurted from Billy's left thigh, running down his pants leg and into his boot. He quickly hobbled away, unable to retreive his rifle. Shooting all the while he ducked behind the corrals and ran through the backyards through the orchard to the Martinez house.

When the shooting started, Luisa, the daughter, had been kneading *masa* for tortillas. She had left off her chore, and had run to the window. Peeking out, flour on her hands, she recognized Billy now running throughout the orchard. He knocked on the door and she opened it instantly, pulling him inside. After giving him a wet rag for his wound which appeared to be minor, she hid him in the large flour barrel which was nearly empty, closed the lid, and continued to work her masa.

When the deputies and some soldiers from Fort Stanton arrived, her father Atanacio Martinez was with them. He had been working in the fields down by the river when he heard the shots, and had rushed into town. Luisa had carefully wiped the blood on the floor, and had covered it with the *saleita* from in front of the *fogon* before opening the door. She told the deputies that someone had knocked, but having heard the shots, she had refused to open the door (she knew there might be blood on the step outside).

As soon as the deputies and soldiers were in the other part of town searching houses, her father and Sam Corbett spirited Billy out of the house and rushed him quietly to Doctor Ealy who was still at the McSweens'. His superficial wound was cleaned and dressed by the doctor, and he was hidden until nightfall when the trio helped him make his getaway.

The other Regulators had left in a big hurry, and as they went over the hill, John Long took one last pot shot at them, hitting Jim French in his left side, wounding him seriously.

Witnessing the proceedings from the safety of the old Torreon was wide-eyed Bonifacio Baca, son of Captain Saturninio, and his friend Gregorio Wilson. The two, who would be able to testify later on, had run into the Torreon when they heard the first shots. They had been playing near the street when the shooting started and had heard Gregorio's father Juan B. "Green" Wilson yell out in pain and call to them for help. The deposed justice of the peace, also known as "Juan Bautista" had been preparing his garden for spring planting when a stray bullet grazed both legs as he ran from the field.

After the excitement abated the soldiers continued their search for the elusive Billy the Kid. They couldn't figure out where he had disappeared to and would eventually have found him if someone hadn't mentioned that he had seen someone running in the direction of the Rio Bonito, all the while limping away. Billy's friends had again come through.

Captain Purrington and ex-deputy sheriff Peppin, (even though his commission had legally expired with the sheriff's death, he was still acting in his former position) quickly formed plans for the Regulators' arrest. Anyone remotely connected or associated with McSween, the Kid or Tunstall was taken into tow.

First to be arrested was David Shields, McSween's brother-in-law, Robert Widenmann, George Robinson and George Washington, Negro employees of Tunstall's. Doctor Montague R. Leverson, John Chisum's houseguest from Colorado, became very angry over the illegal proceedings when they attempted to search McSween's house without a warrant, and called their attention to that part of the Constitution of the United States which provides for protection against illegal search or seizure. At this point Captain Purrington pushed him aside, replying, "Damn the Constitution and you for a fool."

Such contempt for the United States Constitution from an officer of the army profoundly shocked Dr. Leverson and those around him, and he had to reply, "I would not live in a country where such outrages as I have witnessed here today are countenanced."

Purrington bowed suavely and retorted, "Sir, you have my permission to suit yourself."

Ex-deputy sheriff Peppin still urged Purrington for authority to search the house, and Purrington replied, "you have the right to do as you please; I will not stop you," condoning the illegal activities. News of the underhanded means employed by Captain Purrington was destined to reach high places.

The following evening, Dr. Leverson wrote two scathing letters; one to President Rutherford B. Hayes and the other to Secretary of the Interior, Carl Schurz. He gave his eyewitness account of the disgraceful happenings of that day, and the traitorous remarks of the captain. He outlined severe charges against Governor Axtel, including remarks that he was a protector of thieves and murderers, and that the two officers, Smith and Purrington, were in fact the heads of this band of thieves. He attacked District Attorney Rynerson as being a willing tool of the Santa Fe ring, as was the governor himself. The charges, coupled with those against the officers on Indian affairs, were to precipitate cataclysmically a full-scale impartial government investigation. Three days later another of the Tunstall murder posse members would also meet his fate.

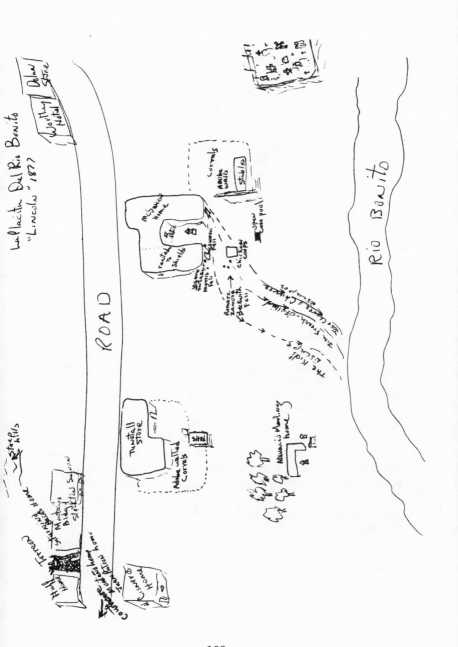

La Placita Del Rio Bonito
"Lincoln" 1877

103

Chapter Seven

Long-Legged Bounty Hunter

On April 2nd, 1878, in a special meeting of the Lincoln County Commission, it was agreed that a reward should be offered for the arrest and delivery to an officer of the law of any one of the men who had killed Sheriff Brady and Deputy Sheriff Hindmann. The amount of $200 per man, dead or alive, was unanimously agreed upon.

Andrew L. Roberts, better known as "Buckshot," was especially interested in this reward. He had been on the slowly diminishing sheriff's posse that had been responsible for Tunstall's death, so he knew without a doubt that he was on the Regulators' list. He figured that since he was being sought by Tunstall's avengers, he might as well hunt for them himself and maybe even make a couple of hundred dollars per head besides. Since he planned to leave the country soon, the money would certainly come in handy.

He rode from his ranch to Lincoln that morning, stopping off at the county courthouse. Checking with the "acting" deputies, he assured himself of the actuality of a big reward. The officers reassured him of this, and glady volunteered the information that the Kid, Waite and Brewer could be found in the vicinity of Blazer's Mill by the reservation.

As he left the courthouse he elicited a few snickers and snide remarks from bystanders due to his rather comical appearance. He made a ridiculous sight with his torn weather-beaten hat pulled down over his ears, long lanky legs dangling over the sides of his short gray mule, almost touching the ground, and loaded for bear. The news of his impending hunt got out fast, soon reaching Billy's ears, when a friend advised him to be on the lookout.

The Brewer party was hungrily ravaging the remains of a home-cooked lunch at Mrs. Godfroy's eating place when they were notified of Robert's approach. Mrs. Godfroy had set up her establishment in Dr. Blazer's building which served variously as his office, the mill, the U.S. Post Office, and the Office of Indian Affairs. He had leased the kitchen and dining area to the wife of the Indian agent Major Fredrick Godfroy to prepare meals for travelers between Ruidoso and the Tularosa.

When they saw Roberts approach, Dick Brewer had to restrain some of his men who wanted to shoot him on the spot, and sent Frank Coe out to talk to him and ask him to surrender peacefully. The Coe brothers, Frank and George, had joined the Brewer posse just recently it was said, after George had been abused and mistreated by Brady and his posse. Brady had heard that at one time Coe had befriended Billy, feeding him and letting him rest up for a few days at his ranch, so he had ridden with his deputies to the ranch and confronted George with the allegation.

"Coe admitted nervously that he had fed him once or twice; after all, he was a friend, but he emphatically denied having taken sides in the present troubles. Brady then told him that he didn't believe him and had ordered his deputies to tie him onto his horse, which they did eagerly, viciously lashing his wrists together and tying his feet firmly under his horse's belly. Every jolt of the horse caused the ropes to cut through his wrists and ankles as they rode to Lincoln, and he had implored Sheriff Brady to at least cut his bleeding wrists free. Sheriff Brady unfeelingly had refused. On the point of fainting when they arrived in Lincoln, he had to be helped off his horse and into the courthouse.

After posting bond, George and his brother rode out to

Billy's hideout, shook hands with him and told him, "From now on Billy, we're with you." Now Frank tried to reason with Buckshot Roberts, whom he knew quite well. He assured him that he would be protected after arrest, and delivered to the proper authorities for his part in the Tunstall murder. He vowed to him that he would see to it personally that no harm would come to him, and if need be he would protect him with his own body.

"No, I'll never surrender to you," Roberts had said softly; "the Kid would kill me on sight. 'Sides,'" he added, "I know what happened to Baker and Morton." As they were talking, Charley Bowdre, George Coe and Middleton came around the corner of the building. "Get your hands up, Roberts," Bowdre hollered. Quick as lightning, Roberts was on his feet shooting, his rifle gripped tightly in his one good hand. Bowdre shot once, getting him in the belly. Doubled over with pain, the bounty hunter jumped up on the step and staggered into the now empty room. He grabbed a thick raw wool mattress from the bed and threw it on the floor in front of the door. Shooting faster than a dozen men, even with his useless left arm he brought down Middleton with a shot in the chest and with another he cut off Charley Bowdre's belt; on its way the bullet sliced off Frank Coe's right thumb completely as Bowdre retrieved his pants. Billy, who had taken cover behind a wagon, received a minor wound in his upper left arm, but continued shooting.

Brewer had found what he considered the safest cover behind a huge log by the sawmill, and slowly raised his head to see what was happening, when with perfect aim, the desperate man put a bullet right between his eyes, ending the fight. Brewer was dead before his head hit the ground. Middleton, Coe and the Kid survived their wounds, but Buckshot Roberts died the next day from his; a hero among his own, he held the fort bravely until his last breath.

Much excitement was wrought up by Brewer's death. He had been known, liked and respected by the people. In a posthumous statement, McSween said of Brewer: "He was physically faultless, generous to a fault, a giant in friendship, possessing an irreproachable character and unsullied honor; he was kind, amiable, and gentle in disposition. The Mexican and American people held him in the highest possible esteem." To Tunstall's father and sister in England, he wrote:

Seven of his murderers are now dead, two are wounded. There will be no peace here until all his murderers have paid their debt. The whole country is up in arms, but this news is marred by the fact that your brothers best friend, R.M. Brewer was killed; John Middleton, James French, W. Bonney (the Kid), Charles Bowdre, and george Coe were wounded. They are recovering rapidly. I have done for them everything that human skill can do. Some of them are farmers, and you may imagine the actual state of things when they took up their guns. They knew, and so did the whole community, that your brothers murderers would never get their due in our courts.

Flattered, the senior Tunstall came through with a large reward for the rest of his son's killers. McSween soon posted the reward notice in the newspaper. It read:

$5,000 REWARD

I am authorized by J.P. Tunstall of London, England, to offer the above reward for the apprehension and conviction of the murderers of his son John H. Tunstall at Lincoln County, New Mexico, on the eighteenth day of February, 1878. The actual murderers are about twenty in number, and I will pay a proportionate sum for the apprehension and conviction of any of them.

A.A. McSween

Lincoln, N.M.
April 17, 1878

Coming immediately after a decisive victory for McSween and his cohorts in district court, the reward offer was expected to bring some action. The hearing scheduled for

April 8th, started instead on the tenth due to Judge Warren Bristol's late arrival.

His first act upon convening was to fill the vacancy in the sheriff's office. He appointed John Copeland to succeed the deceased Brady, probably with the intent of balancing and securing the lopsided leadership of the county. Seventeen days later the county commissioners realized that they had to ratify the appointment, and in a special meeting unanimously appointed him to the office. For more than thirty days, the appointment was a thorn in the side of the Dolan faction. Copeland was proving to be a very active and impartial sheriff, arresting Dolan's men right and left including Dolan himself.

When on May first, Frank McNabb, Abe Sanders and Frank Coe were ambushed and McNabb killed, Copeland had procured warrants through J.G. Trujillo, justice of the peace at San Patricio, and had proceeded to arrest the killers at Fort Stanton where they were being harbored and abetted by the military. In the same period he had arrested three of McSween's men for minor acts of disturbance, and had dealt with them firmly. His reign of impartiality and justice, however, was not destined to last long; on the twenty-eighth of May, through the urging and influence of T.B. Catron who wrote him a long letter, Governor Axtel had him removed. His proclamation again addressed to the citizens of the county dropped a bombshell. It read in part: "John H. Copeland, appointed sheriff by the county commissioners, having failed for more than thirty days to file his bond as collector of taxes, is hereby removed from office of sheriff and I have appointed George W. Peppin, Esq. sheriff of Lincoln County." With the short, loosely worded proclamation, the easily manipulated Governor has again returned power to the ring and the Dolan machine.

Dolan had suffered several indignities and humilities at the hands of Copeland, and when the grand jury indicted Matthews and him as accessories to the Tunstall murder, it was adding insult to injury; his anger knew no bounds. He was placed under a two thousand dollar bond which he quickly posted, and was released. True bills were also found against Evans, Frank Rivers, George Davis, and Miguel

Segura, with indictments of murder placed against the four. Billy Bonney, Fred Waite, Henry Brown and Middleton were indicted for the Brady and Hindmann killings. In the death of Buckshot Roberts only one indictment was found, and it was against Charlie Bowdre.

No indictments were found against McSween or any of his four employees arrested on April first after Brady's killing. Shields Widenmann, Washington and Robinson, still in jail, were subsequently released. Surprisingly, indictments were found against Dolan and Riley for cattle stealing and the purchase of stolen cattle, their main livelihood.

With Peppin's appointment as sheriff, power again shifted to the Dolan side. Immediately, they made plans to arrest as many of the Regulators as they could, and kill those who wouldn't surrender. Peppin appointed a new group of deputies, including many of the villainous old Brady bunch, with a few worse additions. Among them were Marion Turner, John Long, Buck Powell and Jose Chavez y Baca from Lincoln.

Peppin's intention was to execute many of the old warrants including the federal ones since with Catron's help he had also obtained the appointment of U.S. Marshall. His ace in the hole was that now he would be able to obtain aid from the military to execute the warrants. His first request a few days later was for back up support to surround McSween's house and Issac Ellis's store where the Regulators were now headquartered. Several days after that a detachment of soldiers under Lieutenant Millard Goodwin met up with the new sheriff's posse, intending to join forces for the campaign. The officer was astounded to see that it was made up of a weirder collection of renegades and *bandidos* than ever before.

Heading an independent posse called the "Rio Grande Posse" was John Kinney, one of the most unscrupulous, most unsavory characters west of the Mississippi. He had been recruited, it was said, by James Dolan on one of his clandestine trips to La Mesilla, and rumor had it that this was when he had put a price on the heads of McSween, Juan Patron and Billy the Kid.

Having garnered an impressive record in the county of

Dona Ana from whence he had come to Lincoln, Kinney soon scored for the Ruedita, killing Frank McNabb at Fritz's ranch. On numerous occasions throughout 1877 he had been indicted for manslaughter and murder, but had never been convicted; witnesses refused to testify, fearing for their lives; others had simply disappeared. At one time there were seventeen cases docketed against him.

With his group, he had taken part in the "Salt Wars" in San Elizario, Texas, where it was believed that he had fought on the "good side," the wholesale slaughter of Mexican townspeople, even though it was disclaimed and denied by other participants. Strangely enough, it was District Attorney Rynerson who first expounded the virtues and efficiency of the Kinney gang to James Dolan.

Fearing that his addition to the Dolan side would prove detrimental to any attempt to restore law and order in the county, Lieutenant Goodwin flatly refused to join their ranks. He would not permit his soldiers to participate in any campaign with the likes of such men, he advised Sheriff Peppin. Peppin, however, quickly convinced him that as soon as they arrived in Lincoln, he would purge his posse of the offensive element, which would be to the lieutenant's satisfaction.

In a show of strength and unity the group rode into Lincoln. As they arrived they were aware of a ghostly silence; not a thing moved in the usually bustling village. As they were arguing in the outskirts, the village had been completely evacuated by the villagers; even the dogs were gone. They could find no one to arrest.

McSween, for the first time carrying a rifle, had joined "Los Bilitos" at San Patricio. After the death of Brewer at South Forks, Billy the Kid had taken complete charge of the gang; no one, not even McSween had contested his new authority; he was now calling the shots.

The Mexican element of San Patricio had throughout the war been sympathetic to the McSween side; they had always been against "Los Grandes and La Ruedita," and were now happy to provide refuge and assistance to the Regulators. Throughout the month of June, the gang would want for nothing in their comfortable hideout.

The people knew who had disturbed the peace of their valleys through greed and an insatiable thirst for wealth and power; they also knew that el Bilito was a friend who had never refused them help and protection. Billy was a celebrity now, invited to dine at their homes while his men had to cook and prepare their own meals. At their *bailes* and fiestas too, he was the center of attraction; a conspicuous figure; "Quite the dandy," someone said. Señoritas would all glance his way shyly, hoping to be noticed, hoping to be asked to dance, lowering their eyes and blushing if he did.

Billy felt quite at home here. These poor humble folk were his people. He would fight for their rights against all the giants, all the wealthy greedy cattle barons, and all the fat-cat politicians of the Santa Fe ring.

On June 27th, after a minor skirmish right in the outskirts of town with some of Peppin's posse, the gang realized that they would henceforth have to use a bit more caution in their daily movements. Peppin had again asked Colonel Dudley for some soldiers to go after them, but the colonel, having seen Lieutenant Goodwin's report, refused. Sarcastically advising Peppin that with a posse such as that, (he pointed with his nose) he had no need for any soldiers.

On his own, Peppin sent a small scouting party to San Patricio, where they had a minor surprise encounter with Billy and his gang. Unprepared, the gang had fled to the mountains but not before one of them took a pot shot at John Long, killing his horse from under him. Furious over the death of his best mount, Long filed charges of attempted murder against McSween and the Kid on his return to Lincoln. It was rumored by some that it actually was McSween who had pulled the trigger. *Quien sabe?*

The next day, on an inferior mount, Long rode into Lincoln, ranting and raving incessantly over his loss.

About this time, Colonel Dudley decided to take matters into his own hands, sending a detachment to San Patricio to try to capture the gang; if they refused to surrender they had his orders to annihilate the whole bunch.

Captain Carrol, with thirty-five soldiers, soon found the outlaws' trail in the outskirts of San Patricio where they had fled when a scout saw their approach. They followed them close behind through the mountains until about noon, and had just stopped to rest up when a messenger arrived from the fort with orders for them to return to camp immediately.

A recent enactment of Congress on June 18, issued from the war department, explicitly prohibited the military from any action in a posse status for any civil cause except those authorized by the Constitution. The news was a round for the Regulators, and probably had the effect of saving their skins. The series of pesky little raids, skirmishes and chases were getting on Billy's nerves.

Buck Powell had attacked the Chisum ranch, with fifteen men expecting to arrest or kill him or some of his men, but had been merely ignored as they peppered the thick adobe fortress with shot. When Marion Turner and reinforcements arrived next day intending to surround them and smoke or starve them out, the gang was gone. Sometime during the night or early morning they had pulled up stakes and headed back to San Patricio.

When he failed to locate them in San Patricio, an angry Turner ordered a search of the whole village. For this job he picked Jose Chavez y Baca whom he figured might be able to get more out of the natives than he could. They went to every house, forcibly dragging out the occupants and otherwise intimidating and insulting them.

John Kinney, as usual directing his own men, would wherever he went, break down doors, abuse people ruthlessly and pillage their homes without regard for law or diplomacy. After the ruthless gang left, men and boys alike saddled their horses and rode into Billy's camp in the hills to join his campaign.

A letter outlining the atrocities the gang had committed was printed a few days later by *The Cimarron News and Press* under the glaring headline: "Lincoln County—The Peppin Mob Robbing Citizens and Destroying Property." Excerpts from the long letter read as follows:

Kinney the Bandit
The Right Bower of Axtell's Sheriff
Lincoln, N.M.
July 11, 1878.

Headed by Axtell's Sheriff and J.J. Dolan, the Rio Grande posse stole and killed horses in San Patricio last week, and at the same time they broke windows and doors, smashed boxes, and robbed them of their contents. From an old woman who was living alone they stole $438. They tore the roof off of Dow Bros. Store, threw the goods out in the street and took what they wanted. [Billy often had his lunch in the store, and Dow had been questioned previously on his whereabouts by both Dolan and Kinney.] Towards women they used the vilest language. Citizens working in the fields were fired upon but made their escape along the river.

With the same kind of deputies in charge, Peppin sent couriers to all parts of the county urging people to join forces with them to help "eradicate this outlaw gang, this menace to our society." His action served greatly to aid McSween's side as citizens surged to his aid. He decided to return to Lincoln and stand up for his and the people's rights; they needed his leadership and were now flocking to him.

As he rode along the Pecos on his way back to Lincoln, he noticed that without a word or a greeting, determined angry men were quietly taking their places alongside him. From the valleys of the Rio Bonito, San Patricio, Berrendo, the Rio Pecos, the Feliz, and the Hondo; from the far reaches of the Seven Rivers Valley they came, one by one falling into place by him, their guns at their sides. A showdown was imminent and inevitable, they seemed to sense. The time was near at hand.

McSween, thoroughly tired of the bloodshed, sick of the charges and countercharges, writs of mandamus and citations, had been about to resign himself to his fate at their hands, but now, greatly encouraged by the people's obvious support, he knew that he would have to continue his fight for law, order and reason. Volunteers continued to swarm into his camp so that by the time they reached Lincoln, he had over forty new members behind him.

Sheriff Peppin in his recruitment drive hadn't fared so badly either. Intimidating, threatening and coercing, reminding some which side their bread was buttered on, he had

113

gathered quite a few men. Many of them were not content with their new status, however; their hearts were with Billy and McSween, but through fear of reprisal they had been forced to go along.

That evening when all was quiet, Billy, O'Folliard, Jim French, Fred Waite, Scurlock and three others stole through the backyards to McSween's house, entering through the kitchen door in the back. Already inside were many others; there was Tom Cullins, Joe Smith, Harvey Morris (a house guest), Ygenio Salazar, Vicente Romero, Ignacio "Nacho" Gonzales, Jose Chavez, Francisco Zamora, David Shields and his mother, Mrs. McSween, and Mrs. Ealy, the minister's wife.

A few hours later, McSween and his contingent thundered into town, right through the middle of town, out in the open. On their way they deposited a group of men at the Montano store next to the courthouse under Martin Chavez and a few others under Juan Patron at his home. They left a few others at the Ellis store and home in the far eastern part of town as well. They would in this manner be strategically located in all sections of the village and on both sides of the street as well. The enemy likewise had picked choice vantage points here and there throughout the village; to the west, the Dolan Store and the Wortley Hotel; to the east the protective old Torreon, the Saturninio Baca home, and if need be, the County Courthouse itself.

On Monday the fifteenth, the rest of Peppin's group rode in, instantly precipitating a lively round of firing. They headed for the Wortley Hotel where they reached their assignments and soon spread out all over the village. Sporadic shooting continued until late in the evening when they all settled down to a long, quiet, fitful night.

Billy didn't enjoy being cooped up in the house; he wanted to roam the village, draw their fire and take his chances.

"Tomorrow," he told his men, "we'll get together with Martin Chavez and Juan Patron and their men and storm the hotel and Dolan's store."

"We'll do no such thing," countered a shocked McSween; "we're staying right here, and we'll fight only if we need to defend ourselves."

"Didn't know we'd come to a quilting bee," Billy mumbled sarcastically.

The strain between the two leaders was becoming more apparent; McSween, the pacifist, wanted to depend on the scriptures and heavenly protection, while Billy, the reckless one, depended only on himself, his sharp senses and his guns. But even before the historic battle was over, Billy would emerge as the sole unchallenged leader of the group to continue fighting the Dolan forces and the tenacious clutch of the Santa Fe ring—a David against a Goliath.

Chapter Eight

The Coal Oil Brigade

The day dawned beautifully over Lincoln County. The sun peeked over the dark mountain ranges to the east, timid and hesitant, fearful of what the day might bring. It seemed to quiver fearfully in its path as the first volleys of the day were fired from the Montaño home. A rooster started to crow to announce the magical birth of a new day—then changed its mind and disappeared.

The streets of the village were deserted, devoid of their usual commotion. Wide-eyed half-naked children peered breathlessly from behind their mother's full length skirts; villagers stayed behind bolted doors while even the dogs and chickens seemed to have been advised of the state of war. No one—man nor beast dared venture forth into the inviting, beckoning arms of the beautiful day.

From within the confines of the timeless mud and rock walls of the Campo Santo the spirits of the villager's ancestors stirred uneasily, invisibly, questioning, wondering.

At the Montaño home, two men had climbed up on the roof, and from their vantage point were commandeering all of Main Street. No sooner did they lay down flat on the adobe mud roof than two bullets whizzed right by their ears, imbedding themselves deeply in the sod. Scampering down hastily, they saw two figures taking cover behind some rocks high over them in the steep hills above the village.

Two of Dolan's sharpshooters had been spotted in perfect strategic locations, about nine hundred yards away as the crow (and the bullet) flies, and would have to be reckoned with.

"Fernando," Martin Chavez called to the other room, "mira, ven aca."

"Si, Patron." Fernando Herrera, a husky, young farmer a sharpshooter in his own right, came in.

"Que te parece," he said pointing up. "Podremos?" His words trailed off. Herrera was already calculating the distance, squinting, his snow-white teeth gleaming brightly under his thick black moustache. "Traime los binoculos," he demanded confidently. He was handed a pair of binoculars and he studied the rocky hillside terrain, then licked a finger and held it up to feel the direction of the mild morning breeze.

Considering themselves fairly safe at such a remote elevation, the two Dolan men, Charlie Crawford and Lucio Montoya, would, before every shot, raise their heads and shoulders clear above the boulders behind which they stood, let go their volley and then duck back down.

Herrera, immediately sensing a pattern in their actions, took long aim, his buffalo rifle resting on the window sill; no one dared breath. It seemed an eternity—while he aimed, then Crawford stood up to shoot. Bang! Herrera's rifle exploded deafeningly in the crowded little room. A hot lead ball shot straight up the hill. Crawford screamed in pain as it entered his lower abdomen, lodging in his spine breaking his back. He tumbled down the hill, screaming in pain 'till he reached the bottom amid a roar of cheers from the Montano house. Fernando Herrera had once again proven his skill and prowess, becoming a hero and a living legend. For weeks after, little groups of men could be seen climbing the steep hill, again measuring the distance, shaking their heads, collecting bets.

Crawford's companion, needless to say, very soon vacated his post, while Crawford lay in the broiling sun, dying of his wounds.

117

At the store Sheriff Peppin had been writing little notes to Colonel Dudley begging for military assistance to put down the lawless mob as he called them, and advising Dudley that most of the men for whom he had federal warrants were at the McSween house.

"If'n you could jes lend me one of your little howitzers, everything would be jes fine," he said. Colonel Dudley had to refuse. The orders from the war department were strict and to the point.

He relayed his communication to the sheriff with infantryman Benjamin "Berry" Robinson: "My sympathies and those of all my officers are most earnestly and sincerely with you on the side of law and order," he wrote. "Up to the present time," he continued, a little halo twinkling brightly over his head, "I have endeavored in all my official acts to avoid in any possible way by expression or deed to act otherwise than in an impartial manner towards both factions in Lincoln County." His statement was far from the truth but he may have been paving his way in case of a future inquiry.

As his emissary neared the Wortley Hotel a shot rang out raising a wisp of dust at his feet. Taking cover, the Negro soldier went to the sheriff's side, handing him Dudley's negative response. Quickly grasping the situation, Peppin scribbled a hasty note to Dudley. It read:

> General:
> I have the honor to acknowledge the receipt of your very kind favor of date. I am very sorry that I can't get the assistance I asked for, but I will do the best I can. The McSween party fired on your soldier when he was coming into town. On seeing him my men tried to cover him, but it was no use. The soldier will explain the circumstances to you. I take this opportunity to thank you for your kindness in the name of all my people.

With a smile, Sheriff Peppin folded it and handed it to the solider for delivery.

Dudley went into action. He called a staff meeting of all his officers, telling them of the attempted murder of one of his soldiers, asking them for their consent to send in some troops, "to protect innocent women and children," as he said.

On July nineteenth, sixty Negro cavalrymen and nine officers marched into Lincoln, ominously pulling two huge cannon between them, followed immediately by an entourage of sheriff's deputies, smug and triumphant, and Sheriff Peppin strutting like a bantam rooster. They weren't afraid to come out in the open anymore.

Colonel Dudley sent a soldier for John B. Wilson, the justice of the peace, and in a rude and forceful manner ordered him to prepare warrants charging McSween and all his men in the house with assault and intent to kill a soldier of the United States Cavalry. Wilson begged off, saying that it was not lawful for him to issue the warrants, and told Dudley that to his understanding only the U.S. commissioner could legally do so. Wilson later said, "He called me a coward and said many other bad words to me."

He finally accepted the affidavits signed by the officers and issued the bench warrants to the sheriff to serve. Strangely, the warrants were never served nor was an attempt ever made to do so. Instead, Sheriff Peppin and nine men went to the Ellis store, ordering Ellis to give them some coal oil with which to burn down the McSween home. Under the threat of death, he let them take all they wanted; some of the deputies grabbing tobacco and other goods from his shelves and counters as they left.

In another part of town, Dr. Appel was on a mission of mercy. Crawford was still lying, at the bottom of the hill, badly sunburned, but very much alive. He was treated there, then transported to the hospital at the fort where he held his own for over thirty days, finally dying on August twenty-fourth.

The McSween house was on fire. Since all attention had been riveted on Dudley who had called McSween out into the street in front of the house and was now lambasting him, Dolan and some men had found it easy to go around the back undetected, and had splashed the doors and windows with the coal oil and set it on fire. Thoroughly doused, the dry wooden windowsills burned vigorously. The added excitement and the cursing of the angry men inside when they discovered the fire was met with cheers and laughter from those outside. Even the "impartial" Dudley and his men cheered the latest development.

The coal oil brigade had been composed of Dolan, John Long, Buck Powell, and a man who was called "Dummy" for some unknown but perhaps valid reason. As they were splashing the doors someone in the house discovered them and started shooting. Dummy quickly ducked behind a solid adobe wall, followed by Dolan who soon dove in too, but Long and Powell who weren't supposed to be dummies, zigzagged through the backyard to evade the bullets. They obviously zigged when they should have zagged, tumbling head first into an open sewer pit hidden by tall grass.

From there it is believed they called time out and sloshed and slithered on down to the Rio Bonito where they washed off some of the offensive fetid matter and were temporarily out of the game.

"El que anda entre la mierda se tiene que embarrar," some wise old man called out from the protection of his walled porch.

McSween, wringing his hands woefully, was going from room to room bemoaning his extensive losses in the fire. The Shields section of the house was already burning furiously.

Billy closed off another room; he got a thick wool mattress, wet it thoroughly with water, then stuffed it into the doorway, temporarily containing the flames in one room and retarding the fire's growth, prolonging their inevitable evacuation. "Just two more hours, then when it gets dark enough we'll be able to escape out the back," Billy counseled a grieving McSween, no longer a leader.

Coughing and with their eyes watering from the smoke, many of the men wanted to quit and surrender and one mentioned it to Billy. "We're not about to quit now and walk out into their hands," he said; "we're staying right here 'till nightfall—then we'll make a break."

Soon they vacated another room, slowly moving along the U-shaped house from the Shields' section to the front, and from there slowly working their way again to the back to McSween's kitchen. As they left a room they shut the door tight, covered the cracks with wet sacks and mattresses until it once more became too hot and they had to move on to the next one. Finally, they neared the last room; the sun, holding back as it approached the horizon, had lost its fear and now wanted to witness the whole affair.

Across town, the Montaño and Ellis homes had been evacuated by the McSween forces. They had taken to the hills, not necessarily out of fear; but since the arrival of the soldiers their strategic location had lost its importance. There was no way they could shoot over their heads and risk the two homes being leveled by cannonfire as Dudley had earlier warned.

The men under brave Martin Chavez included Billy's close allies Bowdre, Scurlock and Middleton, storekeeper Ellis, Juan Patron, the sharpshooter Fernando Herrera, and twenty others.

Mrs. McSween, Mrs. Shields and her children were finally convinced that they had to leave the burning house. They were all crowded into the last two rooms and soon would have to go anyway. Leaving her former showplace home behind, she pluckily stepped out into the street without even a backward glance, seemingly oblivious to the many guns pointed at her. The others were close behind.

As she walked across the street she looked up and stopped; looking straight at Dudley, who dropped his eyes, she secretly vowed that she would never rest until he was made to pay for all the injustices he had committed against them. Within a few minutes she would have even more reason to wish him eternal damnation.

The sun had finally set; it was beginning to turn dark; Billy hustled from one to the other, whispering that the time was near. He gathered them all together and gave them instructions; in a few minutes when it was a little bit darker they would make a break for the Rio Bonito. Even though some of the men were a full twenty years his senior, they all listened attentively and without question; he was the boss.

Flushed with excitement, Billy organized them by the door; his own self confidence bolstered their waning courage. O'Folliard, always said to be the bravest of the lot, volunteered to go first; he was to be followed by Harvey Morris, a law student and houseguest, Jim French, Jose Chavez y

Chavez, and then the Kid. They would blaze the way for McSween and the rest who would follow right behind them.

About 8:45 P.M. his hand on the doorknob, Billy whispered, "Ready?" (Listos?)

"Vamos, patron," Jose Chavez answered. The door swung open with a bang and out they went, yelling wild Indian war whoops for effect, their guns blazing away. As they dashed across the yard, the first to die was McSween's houseguest, Harvey Morris. He fell mortally wounded, about twenty feet from the door.

Like a pack of frightened deer, Billy and the others fled towards the river, dashing to and fro, dodging bullets, shooting all the while. They swiftly disappeared into the welcome refuge of the darkness by the river, each one remembering and thanking a vaguely conceived god, never recalled until times such as this.

Later, Billy would find out that one of his wild bullets had completely torn off John Kinney's upper lip, scarring him for life, and another had similarly marked old man Pearce, passing through his ear. Badman Kinney would carry a personal vendetta against Billy for the rest of his life, and would remember him daily with a burning passion when he tried to sip his coffee or whistle a tune.

A weary McSween, Ygenio Salazar, Vicente Romero, and Francisco Zamora dashed out next as far as the door, did an abrupt about-face and went back in. They had tarried too long.

Soon a voice was heard, calling out to someone, anyone, outside. It was McSween. "We wish to surrender," he said. "Is there anyone out there with authority to accept our surrender?"

"I can," Bob Beckwith said, stepping out from behind the adobe wall, followed by Joe Nash, Johnny Jones, and lastly the not so dumb "Dummy."

As they stepped out from cover, so did McSween and his last three remaining men, their hands high in the air. Suddenly, from some old adobe shacks in the back, where a few McSween men must have remained hidden, came a sudden volley of shots. Bob Beckwith, their compassionate captor, went down, a bullet through his head. The others scampered back to safety behind the wall.

In the exchange, McSween, who had stopped about eight feet away from the doorway, was next to go, five bullets through his body. To his left, fell Vicente Romero and Francisco Zamora, both dead, and to his right Ygenio Salazar. From the old shack, running feet were heard going towards the river. Someone's bad judgment had caused the death of many good men.

Quiet reigned for what seemed like hours. Were they all dead? Was someone just waiting to kill the first one who dared venture out? Finally, Johnny Jones, his gun ready, cautiously left the confines of the adobe wall, stealthily going from man to man; they were all dead or gone. There was no further resistance. Those who took to the river had escaped in the darkness. The three called to Peppin and his men, whooping jubilantly. Amid shouts of victory they swarmed into the back yard, shaking each other's hands and congratulating themselves. They had won—McSween was dead!

Rolling them over with the tips of their boots, they identified the dead, took their guns and valuables. Then they all left for the cantina to celebrate.

That night, what had not burned up was stolen from McSween's house, and the Tunstall store was looted of all its goods and comestibles. Drunken men and even women and children carted off everything of value. And what of the sheriff and his deputies? They were in the back, outfitting themselves with new boots and breeches.

Early next morning, a coroner's jury made up of six Spanish natives was empanelled. They met briefly in the backyard battlefield among the rank smouldering remains of the McSween home.

"I thought you said they was six," one of them said. "'Pears to me, if'n I knows how to count, that there's only five bodies here."

"There was six," a gravelly voiced, bleary eyed man answered, belching loudly; last night's celebration became today's fermentation, smelling to high heaven on his breath.

After a short deliberation sans one victim, the coroner's jury presented their report:

THE TERRITORY OF NEW MEXICO, COUNTY OF LINCOLN

Proceedings of the coroners jury over the bodies of A.A. McSween, Harvey Morris, Francisco Zamora, Vicente Romero and Robert Beckwith, whose bodies were found at precinct #1 in Lincoln County on July 20, 1878; A.A. McSween with five shots in his body, Harvey Morris with one shot in his body, Vicente Romero with three shots in his body and leg, and Robert Beckwith with two shots, one in the head, one in the wrist, Francisco Zamora with one shot in his body. The coroners jury, after examining all the abovementioned bodies, and from the best evidence they could obtain, render the following verdict, to wit:

We, the coroners jury, under oath do say that A.A. McSween, Harvey Morris, Francisco Zamora, and Vicente Romero came to their deaths by rifle shots from the hands of the sheriff's posse, while they, the above mentioned persons, were resisting the sheriff's posse by force and arms, and that Robert Beckwith came to his death by two rifle shots from the hands of the above named persons, and others while they were resisting the sheriff's posse as aforesaid, with force and arms. Beckwith then and there being a deputy sheriff and in the discharge of his duty as such, trying to arrest the parties for whom he had warrants to arrest.

This being done at precinct #1 in Lincoln County, New Mexico this July 20, 1878.

Felipe Miranda   Octabiano Salas
Jose Garcia   Felipe Mes
Maximiliano Chavez   Jose Serna

Coroner's Jury
Citizens of the County of
Lincoln, N.M.

The missing body found by the coroner's jury that warm July morning was soon identified as that of Ygenio Salazar, a very young friend of Billy's. Those who remembered anything after the previous night's binge recalled having left him lying there with the others when they went to the cantina. "He was dead," one of them ventured positively, "I kicked him over with my boot, and he was dead."

"His family must have carted his body away during the night," they all agreed.

By his own account, later given, fifteen-year-old Ygenio Salazar, one of McSween's valiant volunteers, stated that he had been with the last group to leave the burning house and had been running by the back wall close to the house when he felt two bullets tear through his body, one through his right shoulder and one through his lower back. He had feigned death at first when his enemies swarmed into the yard, but must have fainted from the loss of blood and the pain because he woke up about an hour later finding himself alone and in the dark. He dragged himself out of the yard and down to the river, and after washing his face and wounds in its cool waters had laboriously crawled to his sister-in-law's house, three hundred yards away.

The family was in mourning and was making plans to go for the body at daybreak; they were scared half to death but very thankful when Ygenio spoke to them through the barred door. After ascertaining that it was really him, they unlocked the door and let him in. Laughing and crying at the same time, the family took turns hugging and kissing him, until he finally had to push them away.

"Basta, basta," he said to them; "If I didn't die then, I surely will now with all of you watching me bleed to death and squeezing the last drops from my body instead of getting the doctor." Salazar lived to a ripe old age to recount the story of his adventures with Billy the Kid hundreds of times through the years. "No me tocaba," he'd say to anyone who cared to listen (It just wasn't my turn). (Billy the Kid was my friend). Era mi amigo, el Bilito; muy buen muchacho," he'd say wistfully. A few months after his close scrape with death he was indicted along with Billy for their mutual participation in the Lincoln County War.

After their near barbeque in the McSween house, the Kid's gang started to fall apart. They had rendezvoused in San Patricio after their escape and had gone back to their old trade.

On August 5, 1878 they were blamed for the killing of Morris Bernstein, a clerk at the Indian Agency, and even though Atanacio Martinez, the ex-constable who had once been jailed with Billy, confessed to the killing, warrants were still sent out for the gang.

According to Martinez, he was with a group of men who were attempting to track down some stock stolen by Frank Wheeler and his gang the previous week at San Nicolas, and were watering their horses when Bernstein came at them shooting with both guns. He ducked behind a tree, he said, with Bernstein riding around it in pursuit, trying to get a good shot in. Tiring of his, Martinez pulled his own gun out and shot Bernstein at close range in self-defense.

Even though he offered to turn himself in, his statement was completely ignored. Instead, Sheriff Peppin issued warrants for murder against the Kid, Henry Brown, George and Frank Coe, Fred Waite, Tom O'Folliard, John Middleton, Jim French, Doc Scurlock, John Scroggins, and Steve Stevens. Later on, all of the warrants except the one naming Billy were dismissed. Thereafter, every unsolved killing, every political or boundary murder and every robbery was wiped off the books and attributed to Billy the Kid. "Seria el Bilito," they would say; "quien mas."

With this new killing, Colonel Dudley, also ignoring the confession, went into action. Against his previous orders, he sent a detachment of soldiers after the bandits.

James Dolan and Pantaleon Gallegos had arrived at the Indian agency soon after the killing, and Dolan, it was said, had vehemently urged Dudley to go all out after the Kid and his gang and wipe them off the face of the earth once and for all. This killing had affected Dolan more than any other, since Bernstein, a former employee had also been a very close friend and confidant. The soldiers, under charge of Lieutenant Goodwin, had tracked them for miles in the lava beds, eventually lost the trail and had to give up the chase.

In Lincoln, Mrs. McSween was very distressed. She had

received numerous threats on her life and her friends were urging her to leave the country. She had sent numerous affidavits and communications to Washington City (as she called it) attempting to initiate a complete investigation of Colonel Dudley and his connections with the Santa Fe ring. She held him responsible more than any other for her extensive losses and her husband's death, and showed every determination of doing her best to avenge it. Upon receipt of a final warning note, she left quietly for Las Vegas where her sister Mrs. Shields was now living. Joining the massive exodus from Lincoln County which was now in progress, she arrived there on September twenty-third.

Homesteaders by the hundreds were leaving the beautiful country, leaving their homes and shattered dreams behind.

On August twenty-third *The Las Vegas Gazette* had published the following article making notice of the emigration. It read in part:

> Six wagonloads of emigrants from North and South Spring Rivers in Lincoln County passed through Tuesday going north. They were driven out by the lawless element of the section. They had tried hard to take no part of the conflict and preferred to leave rather than take sides. They left their lands, houses, crops, gardens and everything pertaining to comfortable homes.

Big John Chisum had returned to his ranch after a three-month absence, only to tell his ranch hands and family that he too had decided to pull up stakes and return to Texas. After his decision, the large Mormon colony which had benefited greatly from his protection for about a year after he allowed them to settle on his range, also decided to move on. Having been threatened previously by John Kinney, when he was forcibly trying to recruit their young men for his posse, they knew they would now be at his mercy. Without the people to protect their homes and properties, the lawless element now moved in in full force.

From the Texas panhandle and the desert badlands of Arizona and Mexico they came, seemingly by the hundreds; and taking over the now abandoned, comfortable adobe ranches many of them completely equipped and furnished, they proceeded to terrorize those still remaining. Their rampage of murder. Robbery and the previously unheard of crime of rape, knew no rhyme or reason.

The hardened new breed, especially the Tejanos had no feelings for the peaceful Mexican inhabitants who had steadfastly remained. Their roots were deep; besides, they would meet with an equal number of trials and tribulations, hardships and deprivations no matter where they went. They would stay and with the help of God would weather the storm.

On September twenty-eighth after attempting to enter the Ellis store in broad daylight, a group of bandits went on up to the crossroads to McIlheney's store and held it up. Luckily the frightened proprietor and his family were able to escape through the back into the Chamiso hills.

As the bandits led by John Gunter were leaving with their loot, they saw a dozen or more horses in some old log corrals in the back, and nearby four hard-working young Mexican boys gathering hay in the fields. "Ey, joven," one of the bandits called to them in Spanish, "de quien son las bestias?" Already one of the bandits was opening the gate, and Desiderio, one of the youths, realized what they had in mind.

"Quiten se de hay," he hollered; "esos caballos son de mi padre." (They belong to my father; get away from there).

"Atrevido este,'" said the bandit, pointing his gun at Desiderio's head. He slowly pulled the trigger, hitting him right in between the eyes, scattering blood and brains all over the new-mown hay. The other three boys, at first frozen in their tracks, now tried to run, but it was too late—they were all gunned in the back by the merciless, laughing bandits. Desiderio's brother, Cleto, moaned once, raised his head weakly, and died. Next to him lay Gregorio Sanchez, his cousin, and Lorenzo Lucero, a friend. Having finished his own chores, Lucero had gone over to assist and visit with his friends.

"Jose," a woman screamed, "mira lo que ha pasado— hijitos, Cleto, Desiderio. She gave an agonized scream as she saw their blood-splattered bodies and faces.

"Tejanos desgraciados, cabrones," Jose Chavez y Sanchez

cried, shaking his fists at the receeding bandits, tears rolling down his face.

"Madrecita, no mires: o que han hecho con nuestros hijos estos imbeciles, mal paridos; que se los lleve el diablo a los fondos del infierno; animales, imbeciles que a sus desgraciadas madres—Caya, Josephito, ya no digas esas cosas tan feas; no te condenes solo. Ellos pagaran. Debemos de resarle a nuestro Senor y a su Santa Madre que nos de la fuerza—." Her voice trailed off as she fainted mercifully into the dirt.

The atrocious murders, it was said, had been committed by Bob Speaks, who had led the Chisum cattle drive to Kansas a few years back with Billy, Charley Snow, Reese Gobles, William Dyer, John Gross, and Sam Collyer. May their souls roast in hell.

A posse of citizens was quickly formed and for the next two weeks they pursued the killers through the hills, always a step behind, while they continued their rampage of murder and plunder without restraint.

At Bartlett's Mill they brutally assaulted en masse the wives of two of the young workers. Dragged into the Chamisos from their little company shacks, the two young women had been repeatedly raped by the six or eight men. A Mexican vigilante group was quickly organized by the grieving Don Jose Chavez y Sanchez, Juan Patron, and many of the mill workers, and the broken-hearted young husbands. In two separate encounters they managed to annihilate four of the heartless killers. On October third, two days after Billy helped Doc Scurlock and his family move to Fort Sumner, the two along with a few of the former Regulators attacked and killed a few others of the murderous gang.

Besides John Gunter, one of the most brutal heartless murderers to come out of the state of Texas, John Kinney's gang was also roaming the countryside, reaping the spoils of the Dolan victory. Sheriff Peppin, however, refused to pursue him; he had been an immeasurable ally during the five-day battle.

Instead, the sheriff blamed the county commissioners for refusing to finance any more of his "citizens' posses" as the main reason for widespread violence. Having lost confidence in him, the county officials instead appealed to the governor. When he resigned a few months later, Peppin accused the commissioners of never once having seen fit to pay him his monthly wage. He had never complained in the old days when money had been pouring in from Dolan's coffers, but now that the pickings were mighty lean, he had lost interest in law enforcement.

Meanwhile, Mrs. McSween in Las Vegas would not let things die down, and still deeply hurt, had gone to see a lawyer. Houston Chapman, a recent arrival in Las Vegas, had come from Burlington, Iowa, in the hopes of establishing himself gainfully in the beautiful northern New Mexico area. Having just recently hung up his shingle, he of course welcomed Mrs. McSween's business wholeheartedly and had respectfully and attentively listened to her many problems at first; but before she was even through with her story, he was genuinely and sincerely interested in her extraordinary tale. He could not see, and he told her so, how a mere woman could have survived the agonies and frustrations of such a ruthless, multipronged political attack.

One of his first acts in her behalf was a letter to newly appointed Governor Lew Wallace in Santa Fe. Wallace had been made governor of the territory by President Hayes on September 30, 1878, only three weeks before, and was deeply shocked by the statements in the letter. In it, Chapman openly accused Colonel Dudley of criminal responsibility in the death of Alexander McSween and stated that a great number of his actions had been questionable and gravely offensive to many of the citizens of the territory. He was only waiting, the letter continued, for martial law to be declared so that he could storm Widow McSween's house, arrest her and any and all associates found there at the time.

Even though deeply disturbed by the letter, the governor continued to send rosy, "all's well" reports to Washington. Perhaps wondering what manner of hell's hole he had been sent to he asked the president for a different appointment. "Do you not think that I am now entitled to promotion?" he begged.

On November thirteenth, also perhaps to show how well things were going, he issued a general pardon, "for misdemeanors and offenses committed in the said county of Lincoln against the said laws of the territory in connection with the aforesaid disorders, between the first day of February, 1878, and the date of this proclamation. The disorders lately prevalent in Lincoln County in said territory have been happily brought to an end," he lied.

He had not raised a finger to end the disorders, but was now proudly proclaiming peace and quiet. How farfetched and garrulous his statement was would very soon be evident. Besides cyncial disbelief, his proclamation elicited immediate and angry response from non-other that the deeply offended Colonel Dudley. He took offense to the conditions and limitations conferred in the fourth paragraph, which said:

> It shall not apply except to officers of the United States Army stationed in the said county during the said disorders and to persons who at the time of the commission of the offense or misdemeanors of which they may be accused were in good intent resident citizens of the said territory.
>
> Neither shall it be pleaded by any person in bar of conviction under indictments now found and returned for any such crimes and misdemeanors, nor operate the release of any party undergoing pains and penalties consequent upon sentence heretofore for any crime or misdemeanor.

The latter paragraph brought a response from Billy the Kid. He felt that even though everyone else had been pardoned, by the inclusion of that paragraph, he had been specifically excluded from the otherwise generous pardon. He had been spending most of his time now in the area of Fort Sumner, cultivating friendships, meeting girls, and doing his best to stay out of the reaches of the law, while at the same time pursuing his old livelihood, gambling, and dealing in cattle; his loyalties to Tunstall, however, were not yet forgotten.

He had gone back to Lincoln in late December, and right before Christmas had been thrown into jail. After a few hours in the bitterly cold cell, he burrowed through the thick adobe wall and escaped. He wasn't going to freeze to death in the drafty, unheated cell for any two-bit deputy. He rejoined O'Folliard, Scurlock and Ygenio Salazar at San Patricio where they had again established a temporary headquarters. Like Fort Sumner, it was much to their liking; there was plenty of gambling, strikingly beautiful señoritas and gay *bailes.*

They didn't fear the law much since Peppin's resignation, for quiet, honest George Kimball felt, that it was best to let bygones be bygones and he was willing to let things settle down and let people start their lives anew. He also knew of the many injuries which had been perpetrated against many of Lincoln's citizens. Others, too, were trying to patch up past troubles and grievances. A parley had been arranged between the two warring factions for the first day in February.

It was already one full year since the fateful killing of Tunstall had incited the bloody war. Time had flown for Billy—it seemed like only yesterday. A hundred things and almost as many deaths had occurred since then. It was time to set to rest the vicious vendetta which had so profoundly inspired his every waking moment of the last twelve months. He was tired of running, fighting, of hiding.

His sudden desire for peace may perhaps also have been inspired by his strong love of life. So far, he reasoned, he had managed to escape death at the hands of his enemies, but the odds at this late date were beginning to weigh heavily against him. Should his adversaries continue their enmity, he could not escape his fate much longer. Now he couldn't remember why his loyalties were so strong, why they had carried him so far, almost to the brink of his own destruction. The object of his devotion had long faded from his memory.

That early February morning found him walking down the frozen dusty street. Even though a light snow had fallen the night before, it still hadn't settled the ever present dust. At Billy's side were Tom O'Folliard, Scurlock and Jose Salazar. Ygenio had stayed in San Patricio. As they neared the proposed meeting place, Billy's hands automatically felt for his gun, which was always at his side. He was ready to meet with the Dolan outfit—he was ready to make peace.

Chapter Nine

Tragic Parley

Houston Chapman, impatient for justice, had continued to write long, angry, demanding letters to Governor Lew Wallace. His latest, damningly accusatory letter, had taken on the military together with the whole Dolan outfit. He told the governor that his proclamation of amnesty had served only to grant immunity to the Dolan ring, while they, with the help of the military had continued to persecute and harass the McSween men.

Before Peppin's resignation, on November twenty-fifth, he wrote, the sheriff was just a puppet of the Santa Fe ring and Dolan, and continued to permit atrocities by his former deputies against the peaceful citizens. In another letter, he referred to the burning of McSween's house and his violent death, and the part played by the military, then and now, in the continued harassment of his widow.

"Today," he said, "this town was thrown into a panic by two drunken deputy sheriffs charging into town on their horses with their guns cocked and directed at the house of Mrs. McSween (a short distance from her former home). A few minutes later, a detachment of soldiers under the command of Lieutenant Goodwin came riding into town with three horse thieves who had formerly been on Sheriff Peppin's posse, and were brought in for examination by the justice of the peace."

"What I have to complain of is the riotous manner in which the military, sheriff and deputies charge about all over the country, giving unnecessary alarm and anxiety to peacebly disposed citizens. The sheriff's deputies who were with the military were drunk and had with them flasks of whiskey from which they were continuedly drinking, and their conduct was anything but that of peace officers. I have advised the citizens to shoot any officer who interferes with their rights."

Accusing the governor of indifference, and neglect of his duties, he advised him of a proposed mass meeting: "Unless you come here before that time, you may expect to be severely denounced in language more forceful than polite. A decent respect for the people of this county would have caused you to have come here in person and ascertained who was responsible."

Not receiving immediate response, Chapman proceeded with his plans for a mass meeting. Ben and Issac Ellis, Jose Montano, and Irineo Sanchez had gone to him urging him to call off the meeting. He would only be adding fuel to the dying embers and rekindle the fire; besides they added, it wasn't very prudent to irritate the governor.

After the meeting, which created nothing but animosity and was supported by very few of the people, Chapman was obviously singled out by the Dolanites. The harassment and persecution he had talked so much about now became directed at him.

Late one evening he had gone to Mrs. McSween's house on business and was filling out some forms when two soldiers arrived. They advised Mrs. McSween that Lieutenant J.H. French would be arriving shortly on business. One of the soldiers went over to the lawyer's desk and asked if he were by any chance Houston Chapman.

"Yes, I believe I am," Chapman had responded, peering over the top of his glasses.

"I have orders," the soldier said curtly, "to place you, sir, under arrest, and hold you until Lieutenant French arrives."

The lawyer was about to question his reasons when a loud knock was heard at the door. The lieutenant had arrived, quite obviously under the influence of alcohol. He had under tow a young Mexican boy whom he had just arrested for possesion of firearms. He ordered Chapman to place him under oath so that he could question him. Chapman of course refused, telling him that he was not commissioned under law to administer oath, being merely a lawyer.

The drunken officer insisted, using the most vile language imaginable. More to humor him than anything else, Huston placed the young man under oath. This done, the officer began his interrogation of the quaking youth. Understanding little of his questions, the boy did not answer at all, angering Lieutenant French even more. Fiercely, he turned his attention to the lawyer.

"You're the one I'm really after," he said, "and by God I'm going to get you."

Mrs. McSween had interrupted a few times, objecting to his use of such foul language, only to be stopped with a drunken, "Shut your goddamned mouth, Madam."

"You can't talk to her that way," Chapman broke in, taking a few threatening step towards the officer. "Never have I seen such open disrespect for a lady in my whole life as what you display here today, and I am asking you to take those words back and apologize." No apologies were necessary, as Mrs. McSween had fainted dead away; the inebriated officer staggered out into the night.

From all he had heard, Chapman knew he had been singled out. What had the officer said? He tried to remember the argument.

"You are the troublemaker," he had been told, "who is trying to revive past troubles."

His purpose, he thought, was not that but to defend his client and see some justice come into her troubled life. He would continue to help this spunky woman, to the best of his ability. He would fight the corrupt officials who were continuously making her life so hard and tedious, come what may.

Since it was obvious that Colonel Dudley at the fort was harboring and affording accommodations and protection to the same bandits who were plundering, assaulting and murdering the citizens of the territory, the people had completely lost confidence in the military. Even Peppin, after his resignation, had gone there for protection and was still living at the fort.

Billy and his supporters had returned in full force and were now in complete control of Lincoln. Street fights with the soliders were so common that the town was finally put off limits to them. The Dolan men had not felt quite at ease in the village for a long time, but there was something special about today; they could be found in every bar in town, celebrating. Billy the Kid and his supporters were meeting with Dolan and his supporters; today, they were going to mend fences, bury the hatchet and perhaps even join forces in their respective activities.

"El Bilito viene a hacer las paces," was the word making the rounds from mouth to mouth, to many, a development certainly worth celebrating.

The Dolan trio were waiting when Billy, Salazar and O'Folliard walked in. As a sign of mutual goodwill, they greeted each other warmly and shook hands all around. No sooner had the deliberations started than Evans and Billy became embroiled in a violent argument. It was going to be hard for the two of them to agree on any subject. "There is no way I can reason with a man such as you," Evans told Billy, while Billy, uncommonly for him, managed to keep calm. He answered Evans in a soft patient voice, until finally the terms of the peace developed into a fair agreement, and the gangs again shook hands. The bottle of white lightning which had made quite a few rounds during the stormy conference went around once more. "Matala," someone said, as he produced another one.

By the time they left the meeting room, Bill Campbell, with his permanent sneer, was in an ugly drunken mood. He had attached himself to Dolan, and when they were in their cups, they made a pretty good pair.

About noon, the partying group staggered down the street to the McCullum Saloon, next to the ruins of the McSween home. As fate would have it, on the way they met up with Houston Chapman, the lawyer. He had just returned from a business trip to Las Vegas.

His persistent efforts to bring about law and order to the county and fairness and justice for his client had irked his enemies. Strangely, Bill Campbell the newcomer, who should have been the least irritated, appeared to be the most offended. After a short argument, he pulled out his gun and shot the lawyer at close range. Jesse Evans, according to witnesses, shot him more than once in the street where he lay. Oddly enough, Billy the Kid stood by quietly, witnessing everything, and never once went to his aid.

Perhaps it was true, as Governor Wallace's letter to Secretary of State Schurz a few days later attested, "that certain notorious characters who have managed to escape arrest have formed an alliance which looks like preparations for raids in Lincoln County." Had Billy gone back on his former convictions and allegiances, and summarily joined forces with his former enemies? In his letter, the governor proposed a plan of action, "to take them all in": "I will leave for Lincoln today," he said. "General Hatch, commmanding the district of New Mexico, approves, and will go with me in person and direct the military." His plan suggested, "the untiring use of the troops and Indian scouts."

Escorted by seventeen cavalrymen, they arrived in Lincoln five days later, on March 16, 1879. The governor's first orders upon arrival called for the arrest of Charley Bowdre and Doc Scurlock for the murder of Buckshot Roberts and asked for the removal of Colonel Dudley, charging him with the death of several people; the most recent one, Lawyer Chapman. He had witnesses who had heard Dudley state publicly that Chapman would be dead by nightfall.

Relieving him of his duties, General Hatch ordered him placed under arrest and sent to Fort Union, one hundred and eighty miles to the north, to await charges. He then ordered his replacement by Colonel Henry Carroll of New York. Next, the governor ordered the arrest of Bill Campbell, Jesse Evans, Matthews, Dolan and Billy the Kid.

All but the Kid were taken quite easily, and incarcerated at Fort Stanton where the governor soon found out that security was so lax, that Dolan was soon seen walking the streets of Lincoln putting his affairs in order. Angrily, the governor demanded his rearrest and confinement. "If need be," he said, "we will also send him to Fort Union, near Mora, where his confinement can be assured."

Billy's capture, however, was not so easy; the search centered in Los Encinales, close to Las Tablas where he had many friends, and another hideout. The encino scrub completely covered the craggy bluffs and crevices, and natural caves which abound in the area, and which would have to be shared with bears in the winter. Their strong skunky smell gave proof soon enough, however, as to which caves were being inhabited, and Billy would make it a point to steer clear of those. Only in the case of the main cave would Billy evict a groggy intruder: a lasso would be carefully nudged around its head or paw, then three or four of the men would haul it out where another was waiting by the entrance with his rifle. In its stupor, with eyes unaccustomed to the sun the bear fell easy prey. They would skin it, then someone would catch as much of the clean blood as he could in a pan, while the others cleaned and dressed it. If there was a stream nearby they would rinse out the meat before they hung it out to dry. It made the best jerky.

There was always one in the group who was slightly more inclined to the aspects of preparing food usually associated with woman's work, and he would be chosen to work the blood. This meant working the blood with his hands as it clotted, throwing out the tough sinewy *ebras* as they formed, and pulling out any hairs which had fallen into it.

"Te lavastes las manos?" someone would always ask. (Did you wash your hands?)

Afterwards, with a little bit of fat added, he would place it in a skillet at the edge of the fire and add the chopped-up heart, liver and sweetbreads, and fry it until it was thickened; then he would add an onion, oregano and some chili seeds and hearts. The kidneys never quite made it into the stew, since someone usually ate them raw as they came out of the body. The blood mixture, a rare delicacy, known as *asaduras*, is the first thing one eats from a fresh killed animal, and the hungry men would feast to their hearts' content.

Billy's hideout was never located, nor was he ever

apprehended, but late in the evening of March 18, 1879, John B. "Squire" Wilson had a surprise visitor. He answered a knock on his door to find non other than his good friend Billy the Kid standing there. "Hello, Squire," Billy said, with an impish grin. Wilson, even though justice of the peace, had always been sympathetic to Billy's cause, and considered him a close friend.

"Billy," he said in surprise, "come on in. You don't know how glad I am to see you." Then, clasping his hand, he asked, "What brings you here?" The reasons for Billy's visit were discussed that night until the early hours of the morning. They centered mainly on Billy's chances with the governor and the courts should he decide to surrender and stand trial. Even though he was understandably hesitant to commit himself, he made it quite clear that he was not completely averse to testifying against Chapman's killers.

With Wilson's help and suggestions, he composed a letter that night for delivery to Governor Lew Wallace. Hand delivered by Squire Wilson the next day, the letter elicited pleasant surprise from the governor. Billy wrote:

To His Excellency, the Governor,
Gen. Lew Wallace

Dear Sir:

I have heard that you will give one thousand dollars for my body which, as I can understand it, means alive as a witness. I know that it is as a witness against those that murdered Mr. Chapman. If it was so that I could appear at court I could give the desired information, but I have indictments against me for things that happened in the late Lincoln County War and am afraid to give up because my enemies would kill me. The day Mr. Chapman was murdered I was in Lincoln at the request of good citizens to meet Mr. J. J. Dolan to meet as friends so as to be able to lay aside our arms and go to work. I was present when Mr. Chapman was murdered and know who did it and if it were not for those indictments I would have made it clear before now. If it is in your power to anully those indictments I hope you will do so so as to give me a chance to explain. Please send me an answer telling me what you can do. You can send an answer by bearer. I have no wish to fight anymore, indeed I have not raised an arm since your proclamation. As to my character I refer to any of the citizens, for the majority of them are my friends and have been helping me all they could. I am called Kid Antrim but Antrim is my stepfather's name.

Waiting an answer, I remain
your obedient servant,
W.H. Bonney

The governor answered Billy's letter immediately, the answer which he returned with Squire Wilson. It said in part: "Come to the house of old Squire Wilson (not the lawyer) at nine (9) o'clock next Monday night alone. I have authority to exempt you from prosecution if you will testify to what you say you know." Two night later, the two men met. Billy, following orders, was by himself—except for his rifle, cocked and ready. He entered the room cautiously, looking from side to side. Not until he was sure that he was not going to be ambushed, did he relax.

"I was sent for," he told the two men sitting at a table in the back of the room. "I am here to meet the governor at nine o'clock. Is he here?"

"I am the governor," one of the men answered. "Won't you come in?"

"I have been promised absolute protection," Billy said.

"Yes, and I have kept my promise," the governor answered. "This man and I are the only ones here," he replied, motioning to Squire Wilson.

They shook hands; Billy's hand weather-hardened and rough, the governor's soft, well-manicured and smooth, more used to the pen. Like a girl's, Billy thought, controlling a smile that sought escape. His eyes twinkled merrily, evoking a similar response from the governor.

Lew Wallace had been a soldier, but the years in civil service had begun to soften and mellow the fifty-one year old man. In contrast, the windburned nineteen-year-old fugitive was coarse and rough, clothed in dusty frontier garb. Courteous, intelligent and wise beyond his years, Billy nevertheless was as much at ease as if he had been talking to Squire Wilson, or his partner O'Folliard, who was waiting for him down in the draw.

The governor advised Billy that if he would testify and help him convict the killers of Lawyer Chapman, he would pardon him of all his crimes and let him go free. "Governor," Billy said, "if I were to testify against them, they would kill me." As they were talking and attempting to reach an understanding, Campbell and Evans at Fort Stanton were planning their escape. The next morning, with the help of Texas Jack, a soldier at the fort, they would execute their plans.

After Billy shook hands with Wilson and the governor, he left the house and stole back quietly to his horse and Tom O'Folliard. "Thought you was going to stay there all night," O'Folliard said impatiently. They rode back into the hills, in silence, Billy deeply in thought.

The governor wanted to stage his arrest, making it look good, going even so far as taking him in in shackles and leg irons, pulling off the caper at night when he was supposed to be asleep.

What should he do? Billy thought. My life won't be worth a Mexican centavo if I testify. "Hey, compañero," he said to O'Folliard, "me enquentro entremedio de un penasco y una piedra dura."

"What?" O'Folliard asked; he still hadn't been able to master the Spanish language as Billy had.

"I am caught between a boulder and a hard rock," Billy translated. The news of the two killers' escape the next day made the *piedras* a little more *duras*.

Billy couldn't decide what to do, so in another follow-up letter, he told the governor of his reservations. "I am not afraid to die like a man, fighting," he wrote "but I would not like to be killed like a dog, unarmed. Tell Kimball to let his men be placed around the house and for him to come in alone and he can arrest me. It is not my place to advise you, but I am anxious to have them caught, and perhaps I know how men hide from soldiers better than you."

Billy must have been feeling pressure, for his anxiety to obtain absolution at the expense of betrayal was contrary to his character. The new coalition had been formed less than two weeks before, yet today he was ready to betray his newly found partners.

On the twenty-third of March, the governor's plans were deftly consummated. In a mock scuffle he was overcome and arrested by Sheriff Kimball and incarcerated in Juan Patron's storehouse. When the news of his arrest spread over the countryside, friends and supporters from everywhere started pouring into Juan Patron's house. Some brought their meager savings to help with his defense while others offered advice and encouragement, and many a poor Mexican woman brought him the chili, frijoles and tortillas he adored.

Dumbfounded, Governor Wallace wrote a note to Secretary of State Carl Schurz a few days later, describing with awe the strange goings on: "I heard singing and music the other night," he wrote. "When I got to the door, I found the minstrels of the village actually serenading the fellow in his prison. The precious specimen named the Kid, whom the sheriff is holding here in the plaza, is an object of tender regard."

A few days after this awe inspiring episode, Judge Bristol, under the governor's pressure, reluctantly called a grand jury and a court of inquiry to investigate the many charges against the military. It convened in Lincoln on April fourteenth, and Judge Bristol in an impassioned plea for prudence and good judgment in his charge to the jury asked: "Now let me ask any fair and candid man among you if the experiment of redressing wrongs and grievances in Lincoln County by violence—by the rifle and the revolver—by the shedding of blood—has not been thoroughly tested? What are the results of this method? Is any fair-minded citizen satisfied with them? Does he expect any better results by continuing this experiment? Has it paid?"

Many witnesses, including Bill Bonney were called to testify over the next two weeks and on May first the jury

142

returned a record one hundred and eighty-seven indictments, most of them against men previously associated with the Dolan machine. The majority of them, however, would go scot-free after claiming immunity under the governor's proclamation of the previous November.

During the court of inquiry in late May, Billy was called in to testify on his recollections of the Lincoln County War, but most specifically on the activities of one Colonel Dudley during the shooting of Alexander McSween and the burning of his home. During his testimony of May 28, 1879, Billy stated that his real name was William Bonnie, (misspelled by the court reporter) and that he lived in Lincoln.

"Are you known by or called 'The Kid,' or 'Antrim?" he was asked by the judge.

"Yes," he replied.

"Are you known by or called by 'Billy the Kid?' " he asked again.

"No," Billy replied.

When asked about the July 19th episode the year before, he testified: "I was in Mr. McSween's house in Lincoln, and I seen the soldiers come down from the fort. The sheriff's party, that is, the sheriff's posse, joined them a short distance above the McSween house. The soldiers passed on by, then the sheriff's party dropped off and surrounded the house. Three soldiers came back with Peppin and passed the house twice. Afterwards three soldiers came back and stood by the house's three windows. Mrs. McSween then wrote a note to the officer in charge asking him what the soldiers were placed there for. He replied that they had business there—that if a shot was fired at him or his soliders he had no objections to blowing her house up. I was in the back part of the house when I escaped." (He had run down to the Bonito where others of his friends had been encamped. "We all tried to escape at the same time, but Vicente Romero, Francisco Zamora and Alec McSween had been killed, along with Beckwith of the sheriff's posse." After ending his testimony, the Kid was led back to Patron's house, where he was again jailed.

Mrs. McSween, in her lengthly testimony, among other things, accused Dudley of being the direct cause of her husband's death.

On July 5th, exactly one year and a day after that fateful Fourth of July massacre, the court of inquiry adjourned, finding Dudley not guilty of the charges brought against him. Shortly after the acquittal, an angry Billy the Kid, already freed, stormed into Judge Leonard's bedroom at the fort, announcing that before the day ended he was taking the law into his own hands and was ridding the world of Colonel Dudley.

After a long drawn out discussion, he was finally dissuaded from his avowed course by the judge and Las Vegas Police Chief John McPherson who had accompanied him, and was urged by both to leave the territory for good. His life wasn't worth a plugged nickle here, they told him, and while he still could he should go elsewhere, start afresh and live a long and fruitful life. Instead, the stubborn youth promised them that he would try to forget Dudley and all the past county troubles but, he added that this was his home and he wasn't leaving it for anybody.

Two days later, Billy rode out of Fort Stanton, heading north, then northeast, across the Llano Estacado towards Fort Sumner. Something called him that way, a fate which could not be denied, beckoning, luring him towards Fort Sumner. Or was it the soft alluring Celsa Gutierrez whom it was said he loved? Or perhaps Nasaria Yerbe or Abrana Garcia, two other beauties with whom he often danced? Whatever it was that called him that way, it would still have to take second place to his business ventures.

He joined up with his old gang who were in hiding all this time at Las Verandas by the high peaks, and soon they were back at their usual pursuit. Many were the ranchers who claimed losses at their hands. They would steal horses in the vicinity and sell them across the plains, only to bring back stolen cattle to sell to their first victims. Apparently still trying to get even with John Chisum over the unpaid debt, Billy often hit his massive herds. Some time in October they drove off one hundred and eighteen of his stock, and quickly unloaded them in White Oaks.

Ranchers were often pitted against each other, so ill feelings naturally ran high. The industrious gang would steal from one rancher and sell to his willing neighbor who would ask no questions, only to reverse the process a few days later. The ranchers never realized that there would be no thieves if there were no buyers for stolen goods.

At this time and throughout the following year of 1880, Billy would have the services of his constant companions and allies Mose and Sam Dedrick, Billy Wilson, Señor Moore, W.S. Lamper, A.S. Cook, Rudabaugh, Tom Pickett, O'Folliard, Charley Bowdre, Pasqual Chavez, Billy Pruitt and Ygenio Salazar.

Only about half of the gang was with Billy when he rode into the Milnor Rudulph ranch at Sunnyside by the Pecos on January 11, 1880 for the rest had gone on ahead. They had been riding towards their Roswell hideout in the Verandas, planning to lie low for a while until things cooled off a bit—there had been another killing last night and it could bring repercussions.

Chapter Ten

Billy Visits The Rudulphs

Maria Candelaria Trujillo y Rudulph was standing outside in the sun when they rode up to the house. She was not afraid of them, having recognized the leader right away. Even though the day was cold, in the sun it was warm; she was scrubbing clothes in her large wooden washtub (which on Saturday nights doubled as a bathtub) trying out the fancy new brass *labadero* which her husband Milnor had brought her from Santa Fe. She had been at it all morning, laboriously moving the tub every so often, following the warm January sun around the house, and now as she wiped the perspiration from her face, she felt suddenly tired.

She had left the comforts of home in Rociada as a child bride, not quite twelve years old at the time, in 1857, when she married Milnor Rudulph. She had borne him four children: Milnor, Emilia, Matilde and Charles Frederick. Even though they were now in their late teens and early twenties, they still managed to get plenty of clothes dirty.

When Milnor Rudulph had asked her parents for her hand in marriage, everyone, including Maria Candelaria, had been well pleased. It was the accepted custom that the parents should decide in whose companionship their daughters would spend the rest of their lives, and Milnor was one of the most desirable bachelors of the valley. He had been her teacher in school, and was well respected in the community, having been justice of the peace for a brief spell, while running his mercantile business and ranching at the same time.

When they were married in 1857, her parents Martin Trujillo and Juanita Gomez Trujillo had wept at the wedding. Like all parents, they despaired over the loss of a daughter, especially one so young, but by way of consolation they knew that she would be in good hands. He was a perfect gentleman with his "compañerita," as he called her for a long time, and often wondered how long it was going to take for his bride to truly become his wife.

He took her along on one of his many trips to Las Vegas for supplies for the store and invited his mother-in-law Juanita to go with them too. They stopped at his good friend Pierre Dennis Trambley's mill, where the Stadium now stands in Las Vegas, and ordered some flour for the return trip home.

1834—1917

Maria Candelaria Trujillo Rudulph

She gave a lonely youth refuge, and the nearest thing to home he ever knew—at the beginning—later on, he was on his own.

Milnor Rudulph   1826—1887 (A friend of the Kids.)

A young man of twenty-four from St. Cyprienne, Canada, Trambley had just married Ernestina Pinard from Paris, France, in La Cueva in 1858. They didn't know it then, but they were destined one day to be compadres. Their yet unborn daughter Matilde, would one day marry the Trambley son, Frank Leon, also yet unborn.

The day-long trip in the wagon had been tiring, but early next morning found the two women up and around, looking excitedly into the dusty store windows on Main Street while Milnor went about his business. At one store the young bride caught sight of a beautiful doll with real hair and blue eyes which she just had to have. Her mother, looking around to see that no one was listening, reprimanded her sternly and reminded her that she was now a married woman and had to set these childish things aside. Maria Candelaria, to her embarrassment, started to cry.

As it had to happen, at that moment her husband walked by, and finding his compañerita weeping disconsolately, wanted to know why. Thoroughly flustered and embarrassed, his *suegra* finally blurted out the truth. First astounded, Milnor quickly recouped, gallantly took her by the hand, and without another word, led her into the store. Soon, they came out, Maria Candelaria happily cradling the beautiful doll in her arms.

On their way back home, he looked back with a twinkle in his eye to see her cooing at her doll and cuddling it, she wasn't ready yet, he thought sadly. In return, he would receive a reverent, worshipful smile from his bride, and an occasional embarrassed side glance from his nervous *suegra* at his side. Back at home, in a dither of excitement, she held many a baptism and tea party for her toy doll. Sometimes she would sneak into the store, snatch a handful of cookies or candy from the barrels by the counter while her husband would suddenly appear to be very busy as he dusted the shelves in the back.

When the Civil War started, and he professed a desire to join the service, she already felt the pangs of fear and despair of a wife for her man. He enlisted at Fort Union on October 1, 1861 at the age of thirty-five, and was assigned to the third regiment of the New Mexico volunteer army. Soon after, he received promotion to regimental quartermaster and was assigned to the Hatch ranch.

On March 27, 1862, he applied for membership in the Chapman Masonic Lodge in Fort Union, and was accepted. He was sponsored by Frank Phelps and S.L. Pratt, long-time friends, and was an active, loyal Mason the rest of his life. He returned after the war to his mercantile business in Rociada and would often help as a teacher in the public schools. William Keleher tells us in his book *Violence in Lincoln County:*

> Once each year, in early spring, when the first mountain flowers of the season appeared in the Mora Valley, Milnor Rudulph would suspend lessons and tell his pupils about his boyhood years along the Potomac in Maryland, and of a most important occasion when his father took him to Washinton as a small child and introduced him to Henry Clay (1777-1852), a most famous statesman of the day; he would describe in detail how Mr. Clay shook his hand, patted him on the head and used kind and affectionate words in talking to him.
>
> In the later years, Rudulph had a new story to tell his pupils, about an important day in his life in 1880 on which he received a letter from James A. Garfield, President of the United States, inviting him and Mrs. Rudulph to go to Washington and be guests of the President and Mrs. Garfield. The invitation which they had been unable to accept had been extended, Rudulph would always carefully explain, not through political influence but because he and the President's wife Lucretia Rudulph Garfield were second cousins, and had spent many happy hours together in their childhood.

Lucretia had met and married her teacher, Mr. Garfield, in 1857/1858 when he was president of the Eclectic Institute now known as Hiram College in Ohio. Both were active in literary societies, read, dined, made social calls together, and together virtually ran an intellectual White House. Although she never particularly enjoyed being first lady, she made a good one.

Garfield once said, "Crete," (his nickname for her) "grows up to every new emergency with fine tact and faultless taste." On his way to visit Lucretia who was ill in New Jersey, he was shot. Charles Guiteau, a disappointed office seeker shot him on July 2, 1881, and for the trying eleven weeks that he hovered between life and death, Lucretia stuck faithfully by his side. He died on September 19, 1881, at Elberon, New Jersey.

President James A. Garfield
1831—1881

Shot and wounded a few days before Billy the Kid was killed by Sheriff Pat Garrett!

(Original photo owned by L.L. Branch.)

153

In 1869 Rudulph was appointed postmaster at Rociada by newly elected Republican President Ulysses S. Grant, and in 1870 he was elected to the New Mexico Territorial Legislature in Mora County, serving as speaker of the house that year. He was well remembered for an interesting episode which happened on January 10, 1872. Alexander L. Branch, (the author's paternal great-grandfather,) was Democratic leader of the house, and Milnor Rudulph, (maternal great-grandfather) was Republican speaker of the house. Rudulph had just declared the legislative day ended and had left when Branch called the session back into order. Being the temporary chairman, he appointed John R. Johnson as chairman and left the podium. Now recognized by the chair, Branch entertained a motion that the speaker's chair be declared vacant and named Johnson as Rudulph's successor. His motion was immediately seconded and carried. Johnson then ordered his sergeant at arms to arrest his predecessor Rudulph and two of his most vocal supporters, Juan Chavez and Julian Montoya. He entertained another motion by Branch stating that vacancies existed in the seats of the four Republican members from Taos County, the honorable Buena Ventura Lobato, Antonio De Jesus Sisneros from La Cuesta, Antonio Gallegos, and Juan Antonio Sanchez. They replaced them with a whole new Democratic contingent in the persons of Don Jose Cordoba from Rancho, Juan B. Gonzales and Mateo Romero from Taos, and Francisco Montoya from Arroyo Hondo, giving the Democrats a majority, questionable, in the chambers. Another motion, passed at this time, transferred the Democrats' arch enemy, Chief Justice Palen of the First Judicial District in Santa Fe to troubled La Mesilla.

Managing to sneak a letter out with a visitor, Rudulph called on General Gordon Granger, U.S. Military Commander for New Mexico at Fort Marcy for help. Governor Giddings, recently appointed by President Grant, and just now getting his first taste of New Mexico politics, called personally on the general. Next morning at nine a.m. John R. Johnson, gavel in hand and ready to open the session, was rudely interrupted by a squad of soldiers from Fort Marcy, served with a warrant signed by Attorney General T.B. Catron and placed under arrest. Ten days later the Supreme Court, under Judge H.S. Johnson (no relation to the ex-speaker) ruled that their takeover had been illegal, unauthorized, revolutionary, and declared all actions taken by that body null and void. A strange climax to the story came a few years later when the two political rivals also became compadres—Branch's daughter Carolina married the Rudulph son, Milnor. Needless to say, after that fateful union, their political differences were somewhat toned down and held at bay. This story, and many others on New Mexico's problematic past is very well presented to us by Mr. Calvin Horn in his book, *New Mexico's Troubled Years* the foreward of which was written by the late humanitarian, President John F. Kennedy.

T. J. Curran, SANTE FE. N. M.

Quite the political rascal
Alexander L. Branch
had thrown out all the
Republican legislators from Taos County.

In 1849, twenty-three-year-old Rudulph had been caught up in the excitement of the gold rush to California, and had left his home in Memphis, Tennessee. His mother Marion Wallington and his father, also named Milnor, had remained in Elton, Maryland with the rest of the children when Milnor and his brother John had come out west.

After the long, hard, dusty trek in a wagon, Santa Fe looked like a paradise. Milnor decided to rest up for a few days, but soon, without too much deliberation, decided to stay. His brother, however, went on to the promised riches, only to return a year and a half later.

Rudulph, being well educated, was doing quite well by this time. His education had started in Elton, Maryland in the public schools about in 1832; then the family moved to Memphis, Tennessee where he studied mathematics and the classics. In 1844, at the age of eighteen, he was teaching in the public schools, and managing a mercantile business on the side. His parents had by now returned to their home on the banks of the Potomac in Maryland where they remained throughout their old age.

In Santa Fe, Rudulph was immediately employed in the schools. A man of good breeding and education coming from such far advanced cities in the east was always in demand. He was soon caught up in the newly emerging social circles of the frontier, and spent many an enjoyable evening in the homes of the elite of the village.

On one such an occasion, Rudulph and a teacher friend were dining in the home of a well-to-do Spanish matron when someone knocked on the door. No servants being in sight, the lady of the house was about to stand up to answer the door when Rudulph decided to practice his Spanish. Courteously intending to ask her to remain at table while he himself answered the door, he blurted something out in the still somewhat unfamiliar tongue. Whatever came out must have been terribly insulting because his hostess gasped and nearly fainted; she left the room in a huff, retreating to her boudoir for the rest of the evening, putting an end to the elegant dinner.

Embarrassed to the highest degree, Rudulph vowed to his friend that he would learn good Spanish if it were the last thing he ever did, or else he would never attempt to speak it again. He did so well with his promise that a year later he was acting as court interpreter for the First Judicial District. He went to Rociada in about 1855, marrying Maria Candelaria two years later.

She was now standing under the tall apple tree in the patio, watching the men ride in. Strangers, she thought, to these parts, except el Bilito, whom she recognized immediately. "Bien venido, Billy," she said, "llega, Milnor no esta aqui ahora," she continued, "pero pronto vuelve." He had gone to the south pasture, she explained, to free a cow that was stuck belly-deep in the bogs down by the river. Their neighbor, Arsenio Martinez and her two sons Charley and Minnie had gone along to help.

"Necesitamos posada por la noche, Ma," Billy said (We need a place to stay).

He had always called her "Ma," perhaps in jest over the Spanish custom of abbreviating the first name, Maria, or maybe it felt good to be able to call somebody Ma.

"You know that you are always welcome in our home, Billy." She had answered in perfect English. While her husband had mastered the Spanish language, and now spoke like a native, she in turn had perfected her English.

She sent them to the bunkhouse in the barn, advising the men to feel free to water and feed their horses as need be, and there were staples in the cupboard for their supper, she added. Turning her attention to Billy, who had just moved her heavy washtub further into the sun, and was now picking up the two empty oaken buckets to fetch her some more rinsing water, she thanked him for his help, "Gracias, Billy," she said, "tu duermes en el cuarto de la orilla, tu sabes donde." He always received better accomodations than the others, and later on would be invited to join the family for dinner, while the men had to prepare their own on the bunkhouse stove.

It was the last time he had been here last summer, she remembered with a chuckle, that he had told them the story of the *baile* in La Placita del Rio Bonito, scaring them all half to death. The children had talked of nothing else for days after, and you could see a little more fervor and dedication in

158

their prayers that week.

Many unmarried people of the village, his story went, had been living in sin, and the married ones were not doing much better. Fornication and adultery had become the norm. The *bailes* had become first-class orgies like those of Roman times, and there was absolutely no shame.

Two sisters, Polonia and Roselia, living close by to each other had exchanged husbands half a dozen times, but this time Roselias latest hadn't attended the dance, being, as she called it, "mas malo que un perro," (sicker than a dog) with a terrible *cruda* from his drinking of the night before. She had danced with Polonia's husband Ramon a couple of times, but the third time had been rudely pushed away. "Look for your own tonight, Vata," Polonia had told her, giving her a sister a withering look.

At that moment, as if from nowhere, a tall, dark, handsome young stranger appeared at the doorway, smiling broadly into the room at everybody. He glanced around the dimly lit *sala*, his big dark eyes quickly finding Roselia. She smiled at him invitingly, lowering her eyes seductively, her blood rushing feverishly through her veins, her bosom heaving excitedly. "I'll get rid of my *viejo* somehow tonight," she vowed to herself. "Este hueso es de mi perro."

She looked up coquettishly, startled to see him already standing at her side. She hadn't even seen him cross the room, she thought frowning, but she soon forgot it as she melted under his bold suggestive gaze. "Bailamos?" he asked with a deep throaty masculine voice that seemed to come from his very depths.

Breathlessly, she barely managed a whispered "si," as he took her hand in his and looked into her eyes she shuddered uncontrollably with a strange fear she couldn't explain, unable to pull her eyes or hand away.

Round and round she went, crushed to his chest, the strange odor of sulphur and dust suffocatingly in the air. Her nostrils were open wide, snorting, lungs gasping for air; the others, fascinated, staring fixedly as if in a trance, mouths gaping.

The crescendo of the music rising to a feverish pitch, her fingers dug deeply into his hairy shoulder, drawing blood;

159

then suddenly a piercing scream. The music stopped. A chubby woman screamed shrilly, again and again, unable to stop; a trembling finger pointed shakily to his rump. A tail—a long black hairy tail had fallen out over his belt and pants. His shoes fell off, then all could see his cloven feet, hooves of a goat, *"el diablo,"* someone screamed; *"satanas!"*

"Ave Maria purisima; Jesus, Maria y Jose; alaben los santos nombres," all screamed in fear, calling on the God they had forsaken until now.

Startled, he stood in the center of the room, an animal, caged, snarling, long nails ready, lashing, saliva foaming at the mouth; and then the holy words. A groan, a scream emerging painfully from his animal throat. Then an explosion, a smelly black sulphur cloud and he was gone. . .

Pandemonium finally abated, the shaking dancers looked fearfully down to the floor through the dust; there was Roselia, dead, a fist full of bloody animal hair clutched tightly in her hand, fear-filled eyes wide open, unseeing, staring frightfully at the crowd. El diablo had claimed his bride. Needless to say, the lone church with the big campana in the placita did a thriving business for weeks and weeks after the scare he'd finished.

Muy Christoso, she thought, always smiling, always laughing, *puro Chivito*. He couldn't scare her with his ghosts and *brujas*, and now *diablos*. There was no such thing, she thought, suddenly shivering, quickly glancing over her shoulder.

Her mind quickly jumped to an incident which had happened on one of her visits back to Rociada. Something had scared her half to death then, the night she saw the light. Even though she tried not to believe in their existence, she knew that there were powerful, evil forces in the world which were hard to explain.

It was the fourth year of her marriage to Milnor when she had made the long, torturous trip back to the mountains of Rociada, not only for pleasure, but also to help her mother who had fallen ill. The doctor didn't really know what it was, but had diagnosed it as consumption. Everybody's sicknesses nowadays was consumption, she thought drily as she wrapped up the hot brick she had warmed in the oven to put under her mother's cold feet.

It was about the third night she had been there that she saw the strange light. She heard the owls hooting every night in the trees, but on this particular night, there seemed to be many more of them, or they were much closer to the house than usual. Chills went up and down her spine. Owls had always scared her since she was little, because people always said that they were *brujas* in disguise, devil witches that with the evil power of *la piedra humana* could change to owls at midnight during a full moon.

That night, to be closer to her mother in case she needed her and since her father was away in Wyoming, Maria Candelaria slept in the same bed with her. She had fixed her a cup of *atole* then retired for the night.

She still hadn't been able to fall asleep, and her mother was sleeping fitfully when she saw it. There was a big full moon that night, and she was happy at first that the night was as bright as day, until she remembered the full moon and the brujas and she started to get scared. "Mama, someone's coming with a lantern," she had said, even though it didn't really look like a lantern to her. It was the brightest light she had ever seen. Puzzled, she got up and went to the window, but the light had traveled towards the doorway and stopped there. She couldn't see it from where she was, except that it seemed to illuminate the whole yard. "What kind of a light can that be, Mama?" she asked, "I've never seen a light so bright. See how it shines in through the cracks in the door?"

A breathlessly whispered "si," was all her mother could muster.

Perhaps this was like that electric glowlamp which she had read had been invented by Sir Joseph Swan in England a few years before. It was so bright they said, like the sun, that it even dazzled your eyes. But in Rociada? Electricity? Never!

The wooden door which her father had made, had narrow cracks through which the light filtered in and illuminated the whole room.

"Quien es?" she called out the door, shakilly, receiving no answer.

"No abras," (don't open it) her mother cautioned.

The light appeared to be revolving, turning faster and

faster; they could see it through the cracks. Then suddenly it was gone. She looked through every window of the house in all directions, but could see no one, nor had any explanation for the strange light. Where could it have gone? she wondered. A few minutes later, curious, courage returning, she put on her clothes, telling her mother that she was going out to look around the house. Against her mother's wishes she opened the door cautiously, and stepped out into the yard. She went around to the east side of the house, around the back through the flower garden, and back again to the west side, but saw nothing. She was about to go back into the house when she realized that the owls had stopped hooting; she could feel their beady, evil little eyes staring at her from the trees. She started to look up when a terrible sense of horror struck her.

Her hair stood up on end; prickly jabs of electricity went up and down her spine. It was up there. Whatever the thing was, it was up there, on the roof right above the doorway, over her head, peering down at her. She stood there frozen, transfixed, refusing to look up; it seemed an eternity. The back of her neck tingling with horror; the malevolent evil influence above her perched on the flat dirt roof, waiting, watching her. "Dios Ayudame!" she pleaded.

Finally, summoning all her strength and will power, she broke away from the horror and stumbled into the house. Not wanting to scare her mother any further, she didn't tell her of her terrible experience, but quickly bolted her doors.

Afterwards, rosary in hand, she lay there praying, the unanswered question repeating itself in her mind: What could it have been? What horrible, evil force was it that had been sitting there right above her head, practically raising her off her feet with its power?

Her long hair, which she loosened from its normal bun at night must have been standing straight up on end, like a cat's when it gets mad or scared, she thought, stifling a nervous giggle.

"I should have had a mirror; I wonder what I looked like? Then I could have turned the mirror on the darn thing and let it scare itself to death." She stuffed the bed sheet into her mouth, the bed was shaking so with her uncontrollable giggling. It had to be ugly, very ugly; "Oh, my God please deliver us from such horrible monsters." Then the trembling hit her; she couldn't control herself. It must have been a delayed shock reaction. So what the giggling didn't do, the trembling soon did, her mother woke up.

"You must have caught your death of cold out there, Maria. You shouldn't have gone out fresh from the bed, and without your wrap besides." she had admonished her. Maria Candelaria got back out of bed, lit the lamp and took some medicine to take her mind off the frightening experience. She put a stick of wood in the stove to cut the chill and returned to bed.

The strong medicine dulling her senses, she soon slept well. Only once during the night did she wake up. Startled and in a cold sweat, she stared out the window. It was almost daybreak. Witches and monsters didn't like daybreak, she thought, because it reminded them of the resurrection. She had slept well. Billy was coming back from the well with the water she would need to finish her wash. "Muy bajita la noria," he said.

"Si," she answered, "the drought has really affected us this year. Many wells have gone completely dry. The people at the fort have been hauling their water from the river all summer, and their crops finally burned up in the fields without producing much this year. I sure hope the good Lord remembers us this winter with plenty of snow. Pa la primavera."

That evening Billy helped with the chores he knew his good friend Milnor would have to do when he came back from freeing the cow, and was even able to get the men to chop us a big pile of wood and restack some hay which had been blown about by the wind.

When Rudulph came back that evening, he was very happy to see Billy; in fact he was very happy to see him alive—he knew of all the shootings he had been involved in. Arsenio Martinez and he had just been discussing his latest escapade last night in town.

He didn't mention it to Billy, though. He realized that the law of the frontier was kill or be killed, and the one fastest with a gun had a slightly longer lease on life. Billy lived by this law. He knew Billy was fast; he had been trained on the range and could hit a coyote right between the eyes at two hundred yards. With men it was different, however. He had to be quick but also cunning and sly.

Last night at Valdez's cantina in Fort Sumner he had proven that he didn't lack in the last two qualities either. He had been drinking with his companions at the bar when the trouble started. A noisy, loud-mouthed patron had been getting excessively high and ornery and was directing his remarks at Billy. Billy realized that he would have to fight him before the night was over, and had done his best to ignore him in his drunken state, but the man had persisted. On the pretext of admiring his gun, which the stranger had been waving dangerously about all night, Billy had deftly emptied its chambers and pocketed its bullets.

Later in the evening, his courage bolstered by a few more whiskies, the stranger pulled his gun on Billy, rammed it into his chest and pulled the trigger. Surprised, Billy jumped back; the hammer clicked on an empty chamber.

In return, Billy's gun blasted him instantly; the glory seeker or bounty hunter, named Joe Grant, crumpled slowly to the floor, naked horror on his face. "This proves," Billy said as he returned to his cronies, to buy another round, "That if you can't be faster, be smarter."

This episode had happened late last night, Rudulph figured, so it was quite obvious that Billy was making himself scarce should there be repercussions; perhaps this was the reason for his unexpected visit.

Next morning as they helped with the chores before going on their way, a farmhand walked in with a bucket of fresh warm milk from the barn, setting it on the table. It was a foamy delicacy that Billy loved. He had been washing his face at the corner *gomanile* in the kitchen when he saw it. He hurriedly hung the towel back on the rack, threw the basin of dirty water out the door into the patio where it instantly turned to ice, and made a beeline for the milk, dipper in hand. Mrs. Rudulph, who had been watching, stopped him cold. "Billy," she said, "that milk is for the baby."

"I was a baby once too, Mrs. Rudulph," Billy said, pouting, a hurt look in his eye as he hung up the dipper. Yes, she thought, solemnly, he was a baby once too. Someone had loved him, cuddled him, diapered him. What had happened to her? He never mentioned her; was she dead or alive, or did he even know? Did he even care?

After he left that day, Maria Candelaria and Milnor Rudulph pondered wistfully, sadly, on the direction this misguided young man's life was taking. They knew what was going on. He was living on borrowed time.

"El que con mal anda, no espere que con bien no venga," an old Spanish saying came to mind as the band rode off into the horizon in a cloud of dust.

"Vaya con Dios, Bilito."

Photo by Alice Bullock
-1976-

The famous Ceran St. Vrain, Frank L. Trambley—Milnor Rudulph Mill in Mora, New Mexico. Built about in 1864, it was scheduled for demolition in 1975. The author intervened, organized the St. Vrain-Trambley Mill Historical Foundation, Inc., and is seeking funds for its historical preservation and restoration.

Un recuerdo de mi madre Maria C. Rudulph, en ausencia de su hijo y yerno, Minnie y Frank. Dictado y cantado por Calala Trambley.

El dia doce de Septiembre,
Se fue mi amado papa,
Caminando por su suerte,
Dios sabe como le ira.

Me tillito lo acompaña,
Llevando el mismo negocio,
Espero en el santo niño,
Que han de venir con reposo.

Tambien mi querido primo,
Aunque sea muy chiquito,
Todos al mismo negocio,
A poner un molinito.

El Santo Niño de Atocha,
Espero intercedera,
Que encuetren con buena suerte,
Y tengan prosperidad.

Rociada, New Mexico 1904

Chapter Eleven

Back To Business

From their hideout in the four-thousand-foot peaks, they could see for miles in any direction. A cloud of dust would give them ample warning of the approach of a posse or any rider. From this camp, the gang continued their business, trading in cattle and horses, and throughout the spring and summer chalked up more horse thefts to their credit than what "Peg Leg" Tom Smith ever did mules.

Sometime in February, Billy and his gang ran off and appropriated forty-eight head of horses from the Mescalero Apache Indian Reservation. In May, they traveled to Portales, close to the Texas border with a herd of horses, and for their return trip picked up fifty-four head of longhorns from some careless Texans. They then disposed of them quite easily at White Oaks, selling them to Tomas Cooper. Not all of Billy's activities that spring and summer, however, were bad ones. He was also prone to do a good deed every once in a while, and in early April between rustlings he managed to get one in.

John P. Meadows of Roswell told a pioneers' day rally on February 26, 1931 about when he had first met and been befriended by Billy the Kid. Meadows and his good friend

Tom Norris had ridden across the hot dry desert of the Llano Estacado in search of adventure. They had heard of the hot little war going on in the territory of New Mexico, and of the lucrative cattle business opportunities available to anyone there. They had been on the plains a few days, Meadows said, when a strong wind blew off and carried his hat away. He didn't have another, and as a result had suffered a severe sunburn to his face, neck and ears. When they had finally arrived in Fort Sumner, his face, was severely blistered and peeling. In misery, he had dropped himself into the shade behind a building, and was fervently wishing he were dead. Feverish and burning up, he had lain there for quite a while; the shade had moved on, and now, uncaring, he lay in the hot sun, a handkerchief over his face.

After a while, Meadows related, "some fellow come along and give me a kick in the foot, and I took the handkerchief off my face, and he said, "Say partner, you look like you were up against it." I said, "Yes, that's the way it feels." He said, "What's the matter with your face?" So I told him my troubles and about my hat. He said, "You can't lie here in the sun and wind in that fix." I said, "I say so too." He said, "Get up and come on and I'll give you a room and a cot to lay on." I thanked him, and said "I better stay right where I was at."

You see, Tom and me had just crossed the plains and I had got plumb full of creeping vermin, and I didn't want to go to his room and I told him so, and he said, "Oh, I've had a million on me too, come on in." So he picked up my bed, walked in and laid it on an old iron cot that was there. I went in and laid down on it. He went and saw old lady Maxwell (Deluvina) and she was a good lady, and he told her what he had there, so she come over and looked at me. The Kid brought over a sponge and washed off my face and she doctored me back to health again. I think I was about five or six days laying there with this face. That was the first time I met him. I had never heard tell of the Kid, much less seen him before, and finally I began to get well acquainted with him.

Tom come around and said, "so help me, God," I can't find no hat here, looks like they don't even wear them out here." The Kid says, "I'll give him one," and he did, an old Stetson hat he had. So far so good. He and old lady Maxwell kept on feeding me and greasing my face until I got well, and finally I got up and began to mosey around.

Now, the day I got to Fort Sumner, the Kid came in from White Oaks. I got there about nine or ten, and he got there about eleven. He came from Cedar Canyon up to Sumner and I went from Sunnyside down to Sumner. I got to talking with him and the more I talked to the boy, the better I liked him. I didn't care how many men he had killed, I didn't know he had killed any and I didn't care either. I liked him, and I do yet.

But time went on and there was a big fiesta taking place at Puerta Luna, and he said, "I have just come over from White Oaks and I want to go to the fiesta and deal monte to those fellows. I been dealing monte at White Oaks and made some money." Well, the time come for him to go up to Puerta Luna and he had just forty-two head of cattle, yearlings, calves, cows and two-year-olds—I don't know how many of each he had, but whatever it was, he had them forty-two head, and he said, "How would it suit you to work for me a little while." I said, "I'd work for anybody if he would give me something to eat." He said, he'd give me something to eat and a dollar a day if I'd help him take those cattle to Los Portales. That was where he wanted to start a ranch. I said, "Alright, I'll go just so I get something to eat."

So I helped the Kid take his little bunch of cows over there and things didn't look too good to me, not enough of them someway, only forty-two head. And we got there, stayed all night, and the next day he went back and on up to Puerta Luna. I was there and I just don't remember how many days it was, but in a few days a man named Pankey come in. I'll bet a dollar some fellows here remember old Pankey. He lived on Plaza Largo between Fort Sumner and Old Fort Bascom. He was the man and the Kid wrote a note saying, "John, I have sold that entire outfit and brand and all to Mr. Pankey, in case he likes it, and if he does, count it out, tally it out and collect so much—." there was a price on cows, one on calves, steers and so on, and I did just what he told me to do.

Pankey liked the cows and I tallied them out and collected so much; just what the Kid said. I hadn't been there long enough to earn money enough to buy a hat yet and I helped Pankey drive them back to Stinking Springs with his boy, and we stayed all night there, and the next day Pankey pulled out home across to what we called Hubble Springs in them days. That was the way he was traveling and I went on to Fort Sumner and got there between sundown and dark.

I don't believe I ever saw a rougher bunch of men than was in Fort Sumner that evening, and all playing poker and drinking, and there I was with $420 of the Kid's money in the saddle pocket. Uncle George Fulgum was running a little restaurant there, and I thought, I would hate awful bad to have this money took away from me, and I asked Uncle George if he didn't have a cigar box and he dug around and found one, and I put the money in the cigar box with a slip of paper that listed how many cows, how many calves—the tally list, and as I went down in the bend of the Pecos River there was a whole lot of stumps. There was one big one and a bunch of Zaccatone grass growing around it. I slipped that box in there and then went and got a rock and laid it on top of the stump, and went back and told Uncle George all about it. He said, "You acted wise—them men is over in the Kid's room now drinking and playing poker. There must be eight or ten of them and they have been there two or three days now. They were a tough bunch all right.

The next morning I got up and by an hour by sun that bunch of men had just evaporated—I don't know where they went, but they just slipped off and I was awful glad they was gone. The next day, or the next day after that, I don't want you to think I am going to be

171

exact—I might make a mistake in the days—but shortly anyway, the Kid comes in from Puerta Luna. I was sitting on the bench in front of the old man's restaurant, and he got off his pony and asked me about them cattle and I told him, "Yes, I sold them and have got the money down here by the bend of the river." "Well," he says, "what is it doing down there?" And I told him all about these men and he said about who they was—Tom Cooper, Charlie Bowdre, O'Folliard and Billy Wilson and others I don't know who all.

And he says, "I don't think you was in any danger from them," but I found my cigar box where I put it, set it up on the stump and pulled out the paper and said, "Here's how many cattle you had, and here's how much they brought." He went over the tally list and said, "You have got one two-year-old steer too many." "Well, I said, "You got the money and there's no kick coming." "Well," he says, "I don't have no kick, but I didn't have but one two-year-old steer. Well, folks, I run in the long yearling for a two-year-old steer." He kind of laughed, and said, "That's a pretty good stunt and you made yourself a ten dollar bill," and he said, "I'll give you this, you need it, and I think you deserve it, if you can make a cowman like Pankey take a long yearling for a two-year-old, you deserve it."

Well, that brought a warm spot in my heart for that boy and it's there yet.

Soon after this incident, the men rustled a dozen steers from the ranch of John Newcomb on the banks of the Rio Salado, and in early August they were seen driving a dozen bueyes which they stole from Simon Romero four miles south of Fort Sumner. The strong oxen would bring a good price.

As they were planning their next raid, Governor Lew Wallace and La Villa Real de La Santa Fe were getting ready for President Rutherford B. Hayes' visit in October. *The Santa Fe Daily Democrat* continued its year long attack on *The Santa Fe New Mexican*, labeling it the mouthpiece, organ, and protector of gangsters and mobsters, namely the Santa Fe ring.

The coming elections were also causing quite a stir. On October sixteenth the Democrat reprinted a small article from *The Las Vegas Optic*, which read in part: "A citizen of San Miguel County recently bet one thousand head of sheep on the election of Don Miguel A. Otero, and he's a fellow that takes safe bets only." *The New Mexican* was supporting his competitor.

On the twenty-seventh the president, accompanied by General Sherman and a large entourage, arrived. The city was in a dither of excitement as the smart new carriages and ambulances rolled into the plaza. "There is one thing that distinguishes the American from any other nation," *The Democrat* noted, wryly, "and that being loyalty to the powers that be.

"President Hayes has been received by men of all parties with great enthusiasm. We repeat for the time, that the office which he holds was not given him by the voice of the people; that had the lawfully elected man been seated, he would not be visiting our city as president of this great republic."

Regardless of the thorn left in many sides by the decision of the Congress, La Villa Real, a most gracious hostess, received him well and shared of its priceless treasures. "During the day, carriages containing different members of the presidential party were passing to and fro to all points of interest in our city," continued the *Democrat* article.

That night, *luminarias* burned brightly in the plaza and pyrotechnic displays donated by the merchants went off well into the wee hours of the morning. The only thing that dampened the celebration was General Sherman's speech in the plaza the next morning. After attacking Mexicans as being lazy, dirty, and of low esteem, he even managed to attack their eating habits, and clearly stated his opinion of the few remaining Indians. "I have no feelings against the people," he said, "the people sit here and growl and eat their garlic. The soldiers have done all that was possible to clear out Navajos on the one hand and the Apaches on the other, but you might as well try to get rid of snakes and lizards."

His full speech, which caused widespread anger and ill feelings, appeared in its entirety in *The Santa Fe Daily Democrat* of October 29, 1880. Luckily for him another

173

widely used novelty of the area, that of sitting the enemy on a stake, wasn't employed on him that day.

Grocer and rancher Alejandro Grezalachowski was just returning to Puerto de Luna from the exciting doings in Santa Fe, and had stopped to repeat his story to everyone he met when he was notified that his ranch had been wiped out the night before. His ranch, a few miles north of the old fort at Alamo Gordo by the lake had been hit early in the evening by bandits, and not a steer was left. "Los Bilitos," he said angrily, "quien mas?"

Two days later forty-six head disappeared from the Chisum ranch at South Springs and were whisked down to Tularosa by the white deserts overnight. "Bring me all you can, boys," the jovial rancher announced, and sure enough, over the next two months over three hundred head of cattle switched hands from Chisum to the "King of Tularosa."

On their return trip the gang decided to set up headquarters at Verandas by Roswell so as to be closer to their goldmine, the Chisum herds. On November twenty-eighth, the Kid, Billy Wilson, and Dave Rudabaugh quietly rode into White Oaks driving ahead of them thirteen stolen horses. Eyed with suspicion by the villagers, they openly proceeded to confine them to the Dedrick corrals prior to disposal.

They had no sooner closed the corral gates than they were informed that a posse of angry ranchers was being hastily organized to go after them. Billy quickly arranged with Mose and Sam Dedrick to sell them at whatever price they could get and with the proceeds to purchase and deliver a load of food and supplies to them to their other hideout at Las Cañaditas. The gang then sped out of the village.

The Dedrick brothers, believing that the organization of a posse had fallen through since things had quieted down early that afternoon started putting together the Kid's order. Before daybreak, next morning, they loaded their freight wagon well and started for Las Cañaditas, never realizing that they were being followed.

Deputy Sheriff Will Hudgins and eight men were not too far behind, following their tracks, so when Mose left the Las Vegas road and headed for the hills, his destination was readily known. Billy, always alert, saw him being tailed from

174

his post on a little hill, and immediately got his six shooters into action.

In the spirited fight that followed, the only casualties were Billy's and Wilson's horses which were shot out from under them, while they remained unscathed. Their mounts dead, the two scattered into the brush, their pursuers close behind. They were able to make a good stand in the craggy bluffs at the bottom of the hill, soon forcing the posse to give up the fight due to lack of ammunition. The deputies returned to White Oaks empty-handed. Mistaking their quitting for fear, and figuring that they had found a soft posse, Billy, Wilson and Rudabaugh bravely followed the posse back into town next morning.

Under-Deputy Sheriff James Redman had just glanced up to see who was riding into town when a bullet whizzed right by his ear, imbedding itself in the doorway right behind his head. He made tracks fast, finding cover in the Hudgins store, barricading the doors. In a few seconds the streets were full of armed men, angry and anxious to get their hands on the abusive young bandits. Before they could ready their horses, however, the gang was gone. Plans were now seriously formulated to go after the phantom gang, with Deputy James Carlyle in charge.

A dozen men were recruited, some volunteering, and early next morning, this time well equipped and supplied, they rode out of the village. The bandits' tracks, easily found in the dry terrain, were not hard to follow; they had made no attempt to obliterate them or hide their destination in any way.

By late evening they caught up to them forty or so miles from White Oaks at the Jim Greathouse ranch. The long, rambling structure was situated within a large patio, surrounded by high impenetrable rock and adobe walls, and had been built especially for travelers on the old Las Vegas road. It provided fairly good food and comfortable sleeping accommodations. The posse surrounded the ranch house and demanded the outlaws surrender only to be answered by Billys derisive laugh. Soon after, Wilson yelled out over the wall, that they wanted to talk with whoever was in charge.

James Carlyle answered that he was in charge and would

go in and talk to them. Greathouse, who was inside, offered to go outside. Offering himself as a hostage, he walked out into the arms of the posse, while Carlyle went inside to bargain with Billy.

The sun was setting; it set early that time of year. It was only five in the afternoon when it made one last feeble attempt to peek out over the chamiso-covered hills to the west before it sank slowly into the dark mountain range, and very soon after it was dark.

It seemed like hours to the men outside that the discussions had been going on, and from the progressively changing tone of their voices, it was apparent to them that some heavy drinking was taking place behind the formidable adobe walls.

Later, Joe Steck, cook at the house in an interview with the Lincoln County Leader, gave a good eyewitness account of the affair. He said: I found Carlyle under the influence of liquor and insisting on going out, while the others insisted on his staying. I went outside myself. After being out a minute I stopped and turned, when crash! A man came through a window, bong, bang, there was a man's dying yell, and poor Carlyle tumbled to the ground with three bullets in him, dead." Steck and Kuck, who was part owner of the ranch, then fled to a neighboring ranch where they stayed that night, and early next morning cautiously approached the house. "We found poor Carlyle frozen stiff where he fell," Steck said. "We tied a blanket around him and buried him as best we could. He was afterwards taken up and put in a box by the sheriff's posse."

The posse had left and so had Billy and his men, but soon after, Steck said, some posse members returned and set fire to the ranch house, barns and outhouses, and even set fire to old man Spencer's house which was situated nearby.

After returning home and finding it in ruins and ashes, Jim Greathouse went to Las Vegas. Disgruntled and disappointed over his losses and angered because of the newspaper stories which claimed that he had been harboring fugitives, he went to the *Las Vegas Gazette* and demanded to see the editor. Finally, on December third, he was granted an interview to voice his grievances. On the eleventh, the newspaper

176

published his version of the incident.

Jim Greathouse, owner of the ranch where the brush between the White Oaks boys and members of the Kid's gang recently took place, is in Las Vegas. He reports that his ranch was burned during the affair and that he lost $2,000 from the conflagration, including ranch property and general merchandise. He disclaims harboring desperadoes and says the fact that they were there is wholly due to their demanding accommodations. As he kept a public hostelry he could not refuse. He had seen Billy the Kid several times, but did not know either Ruduabaugh or Wilson.

A few days later Pat Garrett, denounced the article, claiming that Jim Greathouse had been an outlaw and that he had worked with Billy Wilson on the buffalo range in the panhandle country, and knew him well.

The Gazette had been clamoring in its editorials for the people of San Miquel County to unite together, in "wiping out this band to the east of us, this horde of outcasts, this scum of society, forever." Billy, an avid reader, found it necessary to reply, and mailed his response to the article from Fort Sumner, on December 12, and addressed it instead to Governor Lew Wallace. A little round halo must have shown brightly over his head as he wrote the typically badly punctuated, rarely capitalized letter, but whether it belonged there or not is hard to say. He wrote:

Dear Sir:
I noticed in *The Las Vegas Gazette*, a piece which stated that Billy the Kid, the name by which I am known in the country was the captain of a band of outlaws who hold Forth at the Portales. There is no such organization in existence. So the gentleman must have drawn very heavily on his imagination. My business at the White Oaks the time I was waylaid and my horse killed was to see Judge Leonard who has my case in hand. He had written to me to come up, that he thought he could get everything straightened out I did not find

him at the Oaks & should have gone to Lincoln if I had met with no accident. After mine and Billie Wilsons horses were killed we both made our way to a station, forty miles from the Oaks kept by Mr. Greathouse. When I got up next morning the house was surrounded by an outfit led by one Carlyle, who came into the house and demanded a surrender. I asked for their papers and they had none. So I concluded it amounted to no more than a mob and told Carlyle that he would have to stay in the house and lead the way out that night. Soon after a note was brought in stating that if Carlyle didn't come out inside of five minutes they would kill the station keeper who had left the house and was with them. In a short time a shot was fired on the outside and Carlyle thinking Greathouse was killed jumped through the window breaking the sash as he went and was killed by his own party they think it was me trying to make my escape the party then withdrew.

They returned the next day and burned an old man Spencers house and Greathouse also.

I made my way to this place afoot and During my absence Deputy Sheriff Garrett acting under Chisums orders went to Portales and found nothing. On his way back he went by Mr. Yerberry's ranch and took a pair of mules of mine which I had left with Mr. Bowdre who is in charge of Mr. Yerbys cattle he claimed that they were stolen and even if they were not he had a right to confiscate any outlaws property.

I have been at Sumner since I left Lincoln making my living gambling the mules were bought by me the truth of which I can prove by the best citizens around sumner. J.S. Chisum is the man who got me into trouble and was benefited thousands by it and is now doing all he can against me there is no Doubt but what there is a great deal of stealing going on in the Territory and a great deal of the property is taken across the plains as it is a good outlet but so far as my being at the head of a band there is nothing of it in several instances I have recovered stolen property when there was no chance to get an officer to do it.

178

One instance for Hugo Zuber post office Puerto de Luna another for Pablo Analla same place.

If some impartial party were to investigate this matter they would find it far different from the impression put out by Chisum and his tools.

W.H. Bonney

The governor, upon receipt of it turned it over to *The Gazette* where it was published in their paper of December 22, 1880.

On December 10th, Frank Stewart, a private detective employed by the Texas Cattle Growers Association for their mutual self protection, left Las Vegas with a group of about twenty men to help in the search for the elusive Billy the Kid. Pat Garrett, now sheriff, was at the same time putting together a group at Fort Sumner. The two leaders, having communicated, planned to rendezvous at the fort.

Governor Wallace, ignoring Billy's claims of innocence, decided to get into the act. He ordered a $500 reward posted for Billy's capture. It is interesting to note that he omitted the usual words, "dead or alive" in his notice. Did he perhaps still have a certain amount of admiration and affection for Billy the Kid?

His reward notice read:

$500 REWARD

Notice is hereby given that five hundred dollars will be paid For the delivery of Bonney alias "The Kid," to the Sheriff of Lincoln County.

Lew Wallace,
Governor of New Mexico

Santa Fe, Dec. 15th, 1880

Chapter Twelve

No More Bacon And Eggs

Billy had stopped by the Rudulph home in Sunnyside a few more times during the summer, sometimes alone, but usually with two or more of his followers. The last time the family had seen him, he was not alone. He was accompanied by five other, rough, tough, hardened criminals, renegades from the law. Milnor Rudulph had recognized all of them that cold November day that they rode into the ranch. Among them was Billy's constant companion, Charlie Bowdre, who had left his small spread by the Ruidoso and his wife Manuela to apostolate for Billy.

He had been with Billy off and on since about 1877 when he had shot up the McSween home, angered because John Chisum refused to step out and fight. He was there when the Indian clerk Bernstein had been killed at the Apache Indian Reservation; on the posse also when Morton, Baker, and McCloskey were annihilated at Bluewater Canyon; at Blazer's mill when Buckshot Roberts and Dick Brewer had died, and during the burning of the McSween home and his death. In short, Bowdre had followed Billy faithfully through many escapades and shady ventures and would be with him to the end.

There was Dave Rudabaugh, stagecoach and train robber; killer of Deputy Antonio Valdez of Las Vegas in April of that year. He had met and teamed up with Billy after that shooting and escape.

Billy Wilson, of course, was there too. He was a young Texan accused of counterfeiting. He had bought a little ranch and had unknowingly (according to him) received his change in bogus notes, and was now wanted by the Federal Government.

Gregarious and friendly, young Tom O'Folliard, his past record now cleared by the governor's executive pardon, was also in the group. The stocky one hundred and seventy-five pound, happy-go-lucky young Texan, a mere twenty-two years old, would also follow Billy faithfully to the end.

The fifth member of Billy's gang was named Tom Pickett, a six-footer from Decatur, Texas, whom Rudulph had known casually as a peace officer in Las Vegas, and who, reputedly, had been a Texas Ranger before coming to New Mexico.

The actions of the group had been well followed by his former friends, the Rudulphs. The killings and robberies attributed to them were becoming commonplace, everyday news, and more and more ruthless with each occurrence.

Since the ambush of Sheriff Brady, Billy's popularity with them had hit rock bottom. The only thing that had kept them loyal to him all this time was the fact that they realized his original motive had been for elusive justice for the people he had been raised with and loved. They knew that the corrupt power and the ruthlessness with which it was employed by the Santa Fe ring and its Lincoln County associates was no myth. This time, however, together with his gang, Billy was relegated to the barn for the night. Never again would he sample the culinary arts or the simple hospitality of the motherly, loving, Maria Candelaria Trujillo y Rudulph.

That night, Milnor Rudulph, somberly requested that Billy's guns and those of his followers be turned in in good faith for the night. Abashedly, and somewhat reluctantly, Billy collected their firearms and glumly deposited them in Rudulph's hands. Rudulph slept somewhat fitfully with them under his mattress that night, his own guns kept in readiness under his pillow. Billy could no longer be trusted, or for that matter, even condoned. There would be no bacon and eggs that morning!

Los Bilitos woke up before sunrise, fed and watered their horses early, and afterwards saddled them and started out. Not smiling, a disquieting, self-denouncing look in his eyes, Billy looked straight at Milnor Ruldulph as he left, saying: "Mil gracias por todo, amigo-adios!"" The next time Rudulph would see him, he would be lying on Don Pedro Maxwell's floor, a bullet hole through his chest.

At a steady clip, they rode off straight into the rising sun. The family watched them until they were mere black specks on the plain. A feeling of foreboding cast a dark shadow over their troubled minds as Charles Frederick, already at his chores, said prophetically; "We're going to have to hunt him down someday."

They had no way of knowing as they stood there in the warm morning sun of Sunnyside Ranch that fall, that it would be much sooner than they anticipated. One month later they would be embroiled in the inevitable and determined manhunt for their former friend, el Bilito, leader of thieves.

Milnor Rudulph looked around his ranch and its beautiful valley. He wasn't happy here anymore; he didn't like what he saw. There had been too many killings, too much hatred and violence, too much discontent. The land wept sadly over all the atrocities it had witnessed, the injustices it had seen, the despoiling of its very soul. It would be years before it could shake the heavy black shroud from its shoulders, before the birds would again sing gaily in its fields, before the wildflowers would again wave freely in its breeze.

The Lincoln County War had taken its toll throughout the countryside. Many of Rudulph's old friends were now gone, having died under the hand of one warring faction or another, many in cold blood. The crushed spirits of those who lived through it but eventually loaded their wagons and left still haunted their former homes, their dreams.

The quiet valleys had become battlefields, and many a

man's hand dripped guiltily with the blood of his neighbor. Terrorized housewives, many of them with broods of ten to fifteen children, feared daily for the lives of their men. Rudulph's thoughts now wandered more often to the peaceful green mountains of Rociada, to the quiet, simple folk he had known there as neighbors and friends. Maybe John Pendaries would sell him back his ranch. It was just a passing thought but it would remain with him and emerge often into his troubled mind over the next few weeks.

Charles Frederick was a young twenty-six on that cold wintry day in 1880, a brave young man of principles, education and good upbringing so that when he was called upon by Pat Garrett to do his duty for the good of his community he could not refuse. Still unmarried, he had been writing to his childhood sweetheart, Emilia Pendaries of Rociada, and hoped someday to return to the place of his birth, and if he were lucky, to make her his wife.

In 1882, his dreams would be fulfilled. The family would return to Rociada. Emilia's father John would sell them back their former home, and he would also give him her hand in marriage. He would make her his "June Bride" at the Roman Catholic Church in Sapello, on June 7, 1883, at 6:30 in the morning.

She would bear him five children, all born at Rincon, New Mexico, as Rociada was then called. The first one was a son, born on April 19, 1884, and named John Milnor by his godparents, Juan and Matilde Pendaries. The second, Louis Frederick, born on October 16, 1885, would be baptized by Charles' parents Milnor and Ma Candelaria Rudulph. Their third, Richard Warwick, was born on June 30, 1887, by Richard and Margueritte P. Dunne. Their fourth, Maria Guadalupe, was born on October 18, 1889 by his brother Milnor and his wife Carolina Branch Rudulph, and their fifth born on November 9, 1893, would be baptized by Mariquita Pendaries and Robert Dunne.

Charles Frederick Rudulph the author of *La Campaña Sobre Los Bilitos*, written in 1880, died of cancer in 1908 at the old Las Vegas Hospital where the university now stands, and is buried in Las Vegas. His wife, Emilia, terribly frightened of contracting the disease, burned everything he owned after his death, including a priceless, handmade silver adorned saddle which he had had made to order in Mexico. Apparently, his handwritten story, "La Campaña Sobre Los Bilitos," escaped the conflagration.

Emilia had been appointed postmistress of the village about 1885, and was credited with giving the name Rociada its official status, when she shortened it from its previous long name, El Rincon Del Tecolote. Ironically, four years after her husband's death, she also died of cancer.

Chapter 13

The Campaign Against Billy and His Gang

La Campaña Sobre Los Bilitos

(My interpretive translation of
this poem follows)

Los siguientes versos fueron escritos en el ano mil ochocientos ochenta por el Señor Charles F. Rudulph de Puerto De Luna estado de Nuevo Mejico. Estan escritos aqui por este autor conforme feron escritos por el. Se siente este auto muy honrado de ser escojido para presentarelos aqui.

1.

Dies y siete de Diciembre
Pat Garrett nos va llegando,
Pidiendo a Puerto De Luna
Su ayuda que vayan dando.
Que en el Fuerte Sumner se aya,
La gavilla de malvados
Todos ya los conocemos,
Por los Bilitos mentados.

2.

Pronto sale un mensajero,
Con precision a nombrar
Hombres montados y armados,
Y diestros para pelear.
Todos juntos en la tarde,
Estaban listos pa salir,
Porque veian Americanos
Se enpiezan a descabullir.

3.

Toditos se derrotaron,
Pues es gente desunida,
Con no darles ni verguenza
Ver salir a la partida.
Solo Juan Roibal salio,
De esa plaza desgraciada,
Particulares no nombro
Porque seria para nada.

4.

Tambien dos estrangeritos
Sin ser del dicho lugar
Salieron aunque atrasito
Sus vidas a peligrar.
Para que diera verguenza,
A unos ciertos prominentes,
Que hablan mucho de su fuerza
Teniendose por valientes.

5.

A los mas perjudiciados
Pregunto porque no fueron
Ninguno quede agraviado
Pues no es esa mi intencion,
Mas tanto es lo que he hablado
Que es lo que me da razon.

6.

Llegamos a Fuerte Sumner
Cerca de la madrugada,
Para las tres de la tarde
Nos cubria una nevada.
Halli nos dieron razon
Que habian salido ya
Los biles la anterior tarde
Para el ojo del Taiba.

7.

El viejo hospital del Fuerte
Para quartel designamos
Mal lugar para tanta gente
Mas bien nos acomodamos.
Tuvimos la mala suerte
De que Bob Campbell supiera,
De nuestra llegada al Fuerte
Pues hubo quien les dijiera.

8.

Mañana del diez y nueve
Johnny—el de Brazil llego,
Y dijo que ya Bob Campbell
Lo noticia les mando.
Que Pat Garrett con cinco hombres,
En el Fuerte amanecio.
Y iban a venir los Biles
Y esto lo desanimo.

9.

Con repugnancia a Jose
Le hizo Pat que escribiera
Al Bilito una notita
Que al Campbell contradijera.
Al recibirla los Biles
Ir al bosque se arresgaron
Luego tomar su camino
Y descuidados llegaron.

10.

En casa de Smith preparada
Creian la sena supimos
Pero ni nunca esperaban
Lo que nosotros les dimos.
Estabamos desquidados
En nuestro cuarto jugando,
Cuando llego el sentinela
Y el aviso nos va dando.

11.

Toditos nos levantamos
Y salimos al portal,
Unos salen a la orilla
Y otros fuimos al corral
Tom Folliard venia adelante
Pues el era el mas valiente,
Sintio su cuerpo pasado
Con un plomito caliente.

12.

Los que fuimos al corral
Nomas volteamos la esquina,
Vimos un bulto a caballo,
Aunque habilla mucha nublina
Solo al caballo le dimos.
Por su mucha liviandad
Pues no llevo a su jinete,
Mas que al ojo del Taiba.

13.

Alto! Les grito Pat Garrett,
El disputado mariscal,
Cuando llego Tomas Folliard
A la orilla del portal.
El Tomas en un momento
A su pistola acudio,
Pero no tubo mas tiempo
Que en lo ultimo la monto.

14.

Pat Garrett le tiro un tiro
Y el caballo se espanto,
Supimos que iba herido
Por el grito que pego,,
Su caballo lo saco,
A una corta distancia
A donde se fue a quejar,
Pues estaba con mucha ansia.

15.

Ya dirigio su caballo
Pues ya le faltaba su vista
Hacia donde estava la gente,
Toda preparada y lista.
Grito´ que venia herido
Y que ya no le tiraran
Pues venia decidido
Que su persona tomaran.

16.

Ya tomamos el caballo
Y de diestro lo lllevamos,
Bien montada la pistola
En su cubierta le hallamos.
Lo metimos para adentro
Pues ya el defensa no hacia,
Lo tendimos en el suelo.
Porque alli camas no habia.

17.

Su cuerpo fue sepultado
Con muy poca ceremonia,
Y todos lo acompañamos
Pues se nos borro la ironia.
El tiroteo ante dicho
A la tropa de malvados
Sucedio como a las ocho,
Y salieron derrotados.

18.

Pues los de mas compañeros
Que a Tomas acompañaban,
Iban quando el tiroteo
Que nomas alas les faltaban.
Al Taiba se dirigeron
Con un caballo baliado,
Como dije antes era,
De Dave Rudabaugh, el mentado.

19.

El veinte y dos en la noche
Del Fuerte Sumner salimos,
Con un frillito muy crudo
Y al Taiba nos dirigimos.
Nos abian informado
Que otro dia en el mañana,
Se iban a desaparecer los Biles
Para tierra muy lejana.

20.

De la casa de Brazil
La huella vamos tomando,
Salen cada uno su rumbo
Y a poco se van juntando.
Caminabamos dos millas
Siempre su huella siguiendo,
Todo el camino de tul
Era el que ellos iban yendo.

21.

Al llegar a la casita
De piedra que esta situada,
A una legua del Taiba
En una loma pelada.

Al cuidado de Roibal
Dejamos la caballada,
En unos corrales viejos
Y seguimos la abanzada.

22.

Siete fuimos con Pat Garrett
Arrando aquella nevada,
Hasta al ver bien la casita
Y como estaba situada.
Acercamos la casita
Sin tener ningun enquentro,
Y al ver las bestias supimos
Que ellos estaban adentro.

23.

En la nieve nos tendimos
Esperando al ver salir,
A los Biles y su gente
Venimos a combatir.
Nos estubimos tres horas
En la misma posicion
Sufriendo un frio terrible
Y con desesperacion.

24.

Cuando ya aclaro bien todo
Por voluntad de dios padre,
Siete balasos tiramos
Al cuerpo de Charley Bawdrey.
Fue el primero que salio
Cierto sin esperar nada,
A darle maize a las bestias
Pues su signo lo llamaba.

25.

A ocho yardas de la casa
Estabamos agachados,
Esperando que salieran
Los Bilitos afamados.
Ya nos hablaron de adentro
Que Charley queria salir,
Pues sus ultimas palabras
Nos las queria decir.

26.

Pat Garrett les respondio
Que salieran todos juntos,
Con las manos levantadas
Si no, serian todos difuntos,
El Charley nomas salio
Pues tenia malas heridas,
Se dirigio hacia nosotros
Con sus manos devididas.

27.

Ya se abraso de Pat Garrett
Y el hablarle se esforso,
Pero ya no pudo hacerlo
Porque luego fallecio.
Despues de que ya murio
Tres bestias vimos atadas,
Y el silencio aunque profundo
Estaban medio espantadas.

28.

El soltarlas determina
Pat Garrett, y se sento,
Y con dos finos balasos
Los cabestras les corto.
Los Biles al oir los tiros
Empiezan a cabestriar,
Al caballo que quedo
Queriendolo hacer entrar.

29.

Pat Garrett no permite esto
Pues toma una mira curta,
Le dio atras de la oreja
Y cayo en la mera puerta.
Oimos a los sitiados
Estar adentro golpeando,
Pues que ya se nos hacia
Que ellos estaban troneriando
Pero esto ellos no podian,
Y en vano estaban trabajando.

30.

Ya cuando nos levantamos
Del lugarcito tan frio,
Pues por poco nos helamos
Con el estomago vacio.
El compositor se veo
En grande tribulacion,
Al ver sus pies chamuscados
Pero no dejo la accion.

31.

Le toco de sentinela
En la tarde en un barranco,
De la puerta de la casa
Veo salir bandera blanca.
Dio aviso a los compañeros,
Les gritamos que salieran,
Y levantaran sus manos,
Toditos nos devedimos
Mandados por veteranos.

32.

Rudabaugh nomas salio
Con sus manos en el viento,
Lo qual a todos lleno
De indecibible contento.
Nos dijo que ya querian
Todos ellos ser tomados,
Si acaso les protegian
De que no fueran colgados.

33.

Pat Garrett les concedio
Y afirmo la condicion,
Y despacho al mensajero
Aque hiciera precision.
Luego los veimos salir
De aquella afamada casa,
Con sus manos levantadas
Colorados como una braza.

34.

Nos pidieron que comer
Pues tenian buen apetito
Y sed, pues no los dejamos
Que bajaran al ojito.
Frank Stewart y Barney Mason
Y el compositor sacaron,
Las armas y cartucheras
Que en la casita dejaron.
Los Biles al entregarse
Ni un cartuchito sacaron.

35.

Los nombres de los tomados
Quatro veimos que quedaron,
Son un poco arrevesados
Pero presos los tomamos.
Quince eramos los mentados
Que no nos olvidaran.
Nos los echamos a en ancas
Pa traerlos al Taiban.

36.

A dos alli mancornamos
A Dave Rudabaugh y al Bilito,
Con una corta cadena
Les echamos candadito.
De alli me separe yo
Pero una cosa si se,
Que tres son los que llevo
Pat Garrett a Santa Fe.

37.

La tomada de estos hombres
Muy deficil parecia,
Pues vivos no los tomaban
Era lo que el Bill decia.
Si el Bill ubiera sabido
Que habia una recompensa,
El no se huviera rendido
Y hubiera echo su defensa.

38.

Pat Garrett ha sido el hombre
A quien todo le devemos,
Este tan gran beneficio
Que nunca lo olvidaremos.
El hombre chiquito no es
No tiene feas miradas,
No mide mas que seis pies
Con unas cuatro pulgadas.

39.

En fin jovenes reflejen
La maxima del oasquin,
Que ustedes han escuchado
Y tienen escrito aqui.
Todo hombre que recio anda
Su carrera es muy cortita,
Antes que lo piense se halla
Rodeado en una casita,
Como se hallaron los Biles,
Y toda su pacotita.

40.

Despedida no les doy
Porque no tengo ninguna,
Basta con saber que estoy
Muy contento en mi casita,
Aqui en el Puerto de Luna.

The following is my interpretive translation of Charles F. Rudulph's verses, "La Campaña Sobre Los Bilitos," written in Spanish in 1880/1881.

Our Campaign Against Billy
and His Gang

It was the seventeenth day of December, 1880, in Puerto De Luna, Territory of New Mexico. It was a bitterly cold wintry day, and a chilling norther had been blowing through the trees outside all morning. We were in for another snow storm, we could tell, probably to hit us by tomorrow morning. I had just received word that Pat Garrett, our new sheriff, had arrived at the Grzelachowski store, asking the citizens for assistance in capturing Billy the Kid and his gang who were supposedly encamped near the village of Fort Sumner.

Barney Mason had heard a rumor that they had intentions of attending the traditional Christmas Eve dance there and perhaps livening up the celebration a bit. Having many friends there, they were always made welcome at the fort.

The well-known band of scoundrels had terrorized the territory for the last few years, with their indiscriminate plunderings and killings. It was their leader, Billy Bonney, who had ambushed and slain our last sheriff, Brady, and was bragging about having eighteen other killings to his name. He had often been a visitor at the home of my parents in Sunnyside, staying with us overnight many a time.

At one point, I had even considered him a close friend, and well remember the admiration I had for him, but now he had taken to outright murder, and many good men had lost their lives from his guns.

Before Garrett came I had realized that he had to be stopped. He was a dangerous threat to every rancher and citizen of the territory, and many had suffered losses at his hands. Sheriff Garrett appointed Barney Mason to choose those who would go on the posse and to see that they were

206

well equipped and outfitted for the tasks to come. George Wilson and I did not have very much of our equipment with us, but soon horses, guns, ammunition and warm clothing were made available to us all.

From among the men of Puerto de Luna, Mason picked the most stalwart, those known for their strength, valor and dedication, and soon had a handsome group all ready to go.

While Garrett and Mason proceeded to outfit the men, some left for their homes for warmer clothing and supplies. Under one pretext or another they all left for their homes. One moment we were all together, getting set to ride out, and the next moment they were all gone.

We waited for them patiently for a long time, but we could have waited until Judgment Day and they would not have shown up. Never had I seen such an open display of cowardice before in all my life. Some of the most prominent ranchers of the area, who had long bragged of their courage and perseverance had turned tail and run. Without shame they had sneaked off into the night.

I will not name any of these men because it is not my intention to persecute, but I will never forget the cowardly exhibition of so many of my friends and neighbors. Only Juan Roybal went from Puerto de Luna, and I offer his name so that he will be well remembered by the people he did not fear to serve.

I myself had known early that morning when Garrett asked for assistance that I would have to go. Personal fears and apprehensions would have to be cast aside. Shortly before we left, two young strangers who had heard the proceedings and had witnessed the shamful exodus volunteered to go. This act should certainly shame all those *prominentes*, who with their tails between their legs, had timidly run away. These two strangers would risk life and limb to help, even though they were not even from Puerto de Luna. My sole regret is that I never learned their names.

There were six of us all together with Pat Garrett that evening on his posse. Juan Roibal, George Wilson, Barney Mason, the two young strangers and myself, Charles F. Rudulph, from Sunnyside and Fort Sumner.

Juan's brother, Jose Roibal had gone on ahead on Garrett's orders to scout Fort Sumner and see if he could learn something of their whereabouts. While attempting to leave the old fort unnoticed, he had been detained by the two Toms, Folliard and Pickett, who questioned him rigorously as to his purposes in the village. Roibal had explained that he was merely a sheepherder looking for his strays. After a spirited discussion, he was finally believed, his explanation accepted, and he was permitted to leave. "Hijole," he told his companions on his return, "ya me traiba la Sebastiana, que cerca me anduvo."

It was very late when we left that night, and already we could see signs of the storm that was to hit that day. Snow flurries danced around our ponies' ears as we slowly rode towards Fort Sumner, carefully picking our way around the *chamisos* and *nopales* in the cold, clear night. It was close to daybreak when we arrived at Fort Sumner, and cautiously approached the village. After careful observation, we realized that they were not there.

We had checked A.H. Smith's corral for signs of their mounts, but they were nowhere in sight, nor were there signs in the snow that they had been there. Soon, one of the early risers advised us that they had left the village late the previous afternoon and had not returned. They had been seen, he said, headed towards El Ojo Del Taiba.

Pat Garrett decided, at this point, that we would make our headquarters at the old abandoned hospital at the fort, quite possibly the very accommodations that they had just vacated. Even though it was rather small, we did what we could to accommodate ourselves.

By three o'clock that afternoon, the full strength of the storm we had been anticipating hit the area. Snowflakes the size of half dollars cascaded down all afternoon and by mid-evening it measured out to about a foot. It would hamper but not stop our important undertaking against Billy the Kid and los Bilitos. Our campaign would resume early next morning.

Shortly before daybreak, the morning of the nineteenth, Johnny from Brazil's arrived. Their ranch was situated about halfway between Fort Sumner and the springs, the area into which the gang had gone. He notified us that Bob Campbell had already sent the Kid a message, warning him that the posse had arrived at the fort the day before and had rested there that night before continuing our pursuit. Due to the heavy snows, the gang had been heading back to the fort, but upon receipt of the message had changed their course.

Angered by this, Pat Garrett ordered Jose Valdez, a friend of the Kid's, who had been with Campbell when Billy was forewarned, to write another note to the Kid, contradicting the previous message, and inviting them to stop by for supper at Smith's house that evening. Resentfully, and making obvious his repugnance for the task, Jose Valdez finally buckled under Garrett's dire threats and wrote the note for him. Billy was his friend—he felt like a traitor.

Never thinking that Pat's ruse would really work, we had settled down after an early supper to play cards. As we lazed in the warm room by the *fogon*, Billy was riding through the deep snow, straight to our doorstep. Perhaps due to the promise of a good hot meal, the freezing weather, and the belief that we had moved on to Roswell as per our note, Billy was a bit more careless than usual.

Right after dark, they rode towards Smith's house. We soon forgot our card game when the sentinel ran in, telling us excitedly that someone was riding in from El Bosque, the heavily wooded area west of the village. It was very foggy that night, so he was unable to say who or how many were in the party.

As we jumped from the table, some of us ran to the corrals, while Pat and two others stayed on the porch. We waited breathlessly for them to fall into our trap, our horses well out of sight. I saw Tomas Folliard, who, it was claimed, always insisted on riding out front, head straight for the porch. As he reached the far end of the porch, Pat Garrett called to him to stop where he was and raise his hands. Instead, Folliard went for his gun. Garrett, in a flat-footed stance and waiting, was faster and shot first. The bandit screamed out in pain as the bullet tore through his body.

As I turned the corner of the corral, I saw another rider in the dark, took quick aim and shot. I missed the man, who turned out to be Tom Rudabaugh, and my shot instead wounded his horse.

Pat Garrett had attempted to capture Folliard without bloodshed, and had called to him to stop, but the bandit had chosen to go for his gun. When he let go his volley, and the outlaw howled with pain, we knew he had been hit but his startled horse had bolted and taken the wounded man far out into the fields. We could hear him moaning and groaning with pain, begging us not to shoot again, that he would turn himself in. Strange tactics for such a brave man, indeed!

Half blind with the blood and pain, Folliard directed his horse towards the noise by the house and gave up. We picked him up from the end of the porch where he had fallen, and carried him into the house. Since there were no beds, we laid him down on the floor. His guns, we found, were cocked and fully loaded, ready to use when we took them from the holsters at his side. As he wailed and lamented his sad misfortune, begging us to tell him he wasn't going to die, Barney Mason was heard to utter to the valorous cowboy, "Take your medicine like a man, Tom."

All hate and anger left us quickly as we watched his body quake and quiver in death, gasping as it drew its last breath. His shattered wound sputtered out its last drops of blood and then his body relaxed and lay still. We turned from the ghastly scene with queasy stomachs, eager to go on to less gruesome things. Folliard's faithful steed neighed nervously out by the porch; he wouldn't be needing him any more. It was eight o'clock in the evening; the whole, nerve shaking drama played out that night had taken less than a half an hour.

We buried Tom Folliard rather unceremoniously next day with all of his pursuers and a few villagers in attendance. He needed no eulogy; with all of his bravado and valor, he had gone the way of all murderers and thieves.

That night, in the following confusion the remainder of the gang was routed and fled the scene as if they had wings. They were headed towards El Ojo del Taiba. Dave Rudua-baugh still rode his wounded horse. Even though dying, his faithful steed would carry him as far as the Wilcox ranch, twelve, miles away. When they arrived there, it laid its head on its forelegs, and quietly passed away.

A bitterly cold wind engulfed us the night of the twenty-second as we left the shelter of the old hospital at the fort, and rode at a steady clip through the deep snow towards Brazil's house where we easily picked up the bandits' trail. At first they went in all directions, but as we reached El Camino del Tul they all came together and headed straight for the springs. Following them through the snow was a simple matter, on such a bright moonlit night.

At Brazil's, we had received word that the gang was leaving the country early next morning after having realized that this time the posse really meant business. Brazil, who had aided and abetted them many a time before, probably out of fear, was now as determined as we that they should be captured and was helping us all he could.

The night of the twentieth, he had ridden the many miles to the fort in below zero weather to give us a message, and had arrived close to midnight, with ice frozen on his beard. After leaving Brazil's house that cold night, we followed their trail for about two miles along the Camino del Tul where they soon cut across country. We realized then that they were heading towards Alejandro Perea's old abandoned rock house in the prairie, about two and a half miles from Taiba, the only shelter for miles.

A short distance from the house we stopped and dismounted, leaving Juan Roibal with the horses in some old corrals. With extreme caution, taking care not to step too loudly in the frozen crunchy snow, we advanced on the old rock house. As we neared, we knew that we had found them there; three horses were tied outside the door.

Following a dry arroyo bed, which went right close to the house, we were able to advance to within a few yards undetected. There were seven of us with Pat Garrett that cold December morning, seeking good vantage spots in the arroyo. The two youngsters who had volunteered at Puerto de Luna were still with us. They were brave young men who wouldn't back off for anything.

For three long hours, we lay in the deep snow surrounding the house, patiently awaiting daybreak and the waking of the fitfully sleeping men inside. Not a sound was heard in that strange, peaceful stillness of the dawn when the whole world appears to stand still, perhaps in solemn witness to the miraculous birth of a new day.

The first rays of light were sharply silhouetting the dark mountain range to the east when we heard stirring within the house. We were only about eight yards away, shivering and half frozen, when at the first crack of dawn a loose board creaked loudly, shattering forever the morning peace.

My heartbeat thundered in my chest like the noise of a thousand stampeding buffalo. My eyes were straining, riveted to the door, when I perceived a slight movement at the entrance to the house. Then out came Charlie Bowdre noisily, toting a bucket of corn for the horses. He stopped and looked around suspiciously, wary as an old bear smelling its surroundings. At that moment seven shots rang out as one. Charlie dropped his bucket, clutched at his chest, and staggered back into the house, mortally wounded. The corn trickled slowly into the red polka dots in the snow.

We advanced cautiously, and were about six yards away, when Billy the Kid called out, "Garrett," and then, "Pat, Charley Bowdre's got a chunk of lead in him the size of a hen's egg and wants to turn himself in if you promise not to shoot him when he comes out."

"Billy," Pat Garrett answered, "it appears to me that the whole lot of you ought to be smart enough to turn youselves in right now, instead of waiting to get the same as your unfortunate compadre."

As if in answer, Charley Bowdre stumbled out the door, his hands gripping the door jam tightly; then he weakly weaved his way towards Pat Garrett, his wounds bleeding profusely. He tried to embrace Pat, saying, "Compadre, I wish, I wish." They were his last words as his legs buckled under him and he fell face down into the snow. His wishes, never voiced, were probably that he had met with Pat Garrett this day under different circumstances.

The peace and quiet returned momentarily as the stunned

men froze, staring fixedly as the last drops of his blood spurted out into the snow. A horse neighed softly, breaking their trance, calling them all back into action. The three horses at the door pawed nervously at the ground as they seemed to realize that attention had now shifted to them. They had followed four sets of horsetracks from Brazil's after Rudabaugh's horse had dropped on the trail, so one other horse must be inside the house, Pat reasoned. He decided to try and cut them loose, then took careful aim, and with two lucky shots was able to sever their ropes. The two frightened animals took off for parts unknown.

Those who remained in the house now realized what had happened and tried desperately to pull the third one in the door. Pat Garrett could not permit this, so with regrets, again taking good aim, he felled the beautiful black animal with a shot behind the ear. It fell kicking and bleating right where he wanted it at the entrance to the house.

The desperate men inside were now hard at work. They were trying to break out through the back wall. Not until they realized that they were completely surrounded did they give up the task.

It was mid-afternoon when we finally changed positions. My stomach was growling with hunger since we had had nothing to eat all day. I soon realized that it was the least of my worries when I found out that my feet were almost frozen; I could feel nothing in my toes.

It was my turn to stand watch that afternoon and I could barely walk as I looked for a good spot in the sun away from the wind, finding one at the edge of the ravine. I had just settled myself down anticipating another cold night in the snow when I caught a movement at the door. Someone was timidly waving a little white flag through the door. Thank God, the Bilitos were ready to give up. I called out loudly to Pat Garrett and the others who were gathering twigs and pieces of old timbers for a fire as Dave Rudabaugh came out, waving the white flag, his hands high in the air.

He seemed overjoyed to see us and, as if nothing had happened, proceeded to greet each one of us as if his long lost brothers had finally come to pay him an overdue visit.

He told us then that the others wanted to give up too, providing we would guarantee that they would not hang.

Pat Garrett took it upon himself to reassure them even though he knew their fate would not be in his hands. He sent Rudabaugh to tell them this, and five minutes later four shamefaced outlaws emerged from the house, their faces red as cinders, their hands high in the air. Thus, the hard ordeal of the last week had finally come to an end. Our campaign against Billy and his gang had come to a successful end. They were thirsty and hungry, but so were we. They wanted to go down to the spring for a drink of water, but not knowing what they had in mind, and anxious to get back home, we did not let them.

Frank Stewart, Barney Mason, and myself went into the little house for their guns and ammunition. Every gun was loaded, cocked, and ready to use, but they hadn't fired a shot.

We made a fire and prepared some food which had been sent to us from the Wilcox ranch, and shared it with our manacled prisoners.

There were four men of the gang left after the deaths of Tom Folliard and Charley Bowdre.

There was Billy, cheerful and chattering, excitement lighting up his face; Rudabaugh, also joyful and talkative; Tom Pickett, scared half to death, pondering his fate; and Billy Wilson, probably the least to blame, ashamed and uncommunicative.

We trussed up Billy and Dave Rudabaugh together with a short chain and padlock and loaded them on a horse for the trip back to El Taiba. We doubled Pickett and Wilson with us on our horses, and started back.

When we arrived at Wilcox Ranch and Brazil's, Pat Garrett sent Mason, Brazil and myself back to the rock house for Bowdre's body. We started with it for Fort Sumner where we were met by a deranged, lamenting Manuela Bowdre. She kicked and pummelled Pat Garrett until she had to be pulled away. We turned her husband's body over to her, and left it there.

Pat, Barney Mason, Jim East, Poker Tom and Stewart took

off with the prisoners towards Las Vegas. The sun was setting as I wearily mounted my horse for the long ride home.

Many thoughts danced through my head as I rode towards Sunnyside; it had been a job well done. I was happy and content; I felt somehow fulfilled. It had been a hard task, which we had all known we had to do; thanks to God it had come off well, without loss of life to our side.

I remembered that Billy had said before that he would not be taken alive; perhaps if he had known that there was a reward on his head, he would have made a stronger defense. Quien sabe?

Pat Garrett is the man to whom we owe our deepest gratitude and eternal thanks, because without his perseverance and dedication, none of this could have been accomplished.

Our week long campaign had started on the seventeenth day of December and ended on the twenty third.

The people of Puerto de Luna, Fort Sumner and the territory as a whole would have the rare opportunity to enjoy peacefully the holy Christmas season which was about to begin.

As I sit here at home in Puerto de Luna, contentedly reflecting on the happenings of the last week, an old saying comes to mind. I offer it here as advice to youth in general, for it is they who are usually most susceptible to the lures and traps offered by reckless adventure. It goes: "He who lives life fastest, lives it shortest," and before he realizes it he may find himself ensnared in a little rock house on the prairie, as we found Billy the Kid y los Bilitos.

Las Vegas and vicinity—1858

Original owned by L.L. Branch

Chapter Fourteen

Mobbed at Las Vegas and
Chained in Santa Fe

It was shortly before sundown when Pat Garrett, Mason, Stewart, Jim East and Poker Tom started for Las Vegas with their four prisoners.

Not one to harbor resentment, Billy had made a present of his trusty bay mare to his captor, Frank Stewart, remarking that he wouldn't have much time to ride her where he was going and he knew Frank would take good care of her. It must have been the hardest thing in the world for Billy to do since he had loved and cared for his animal well since its acquisition two years before. It had carried him faithfully through so many scrapes and escapades that it would unquestionably be missed.

The group reached Gayharts ranch at Arroyo Hondo close to midnight and was given accommodations for the night. After breakfast next morning they started for Puerto de Luna, arriving there about two in the afternoon. It was Christmas Day, 1880, and the home of Alexander Grzelachowski was full of Christmas cheer and holiday spirit. A big dinner had been prepared and was waiting, so without hesitation the affluent merchant joyfully invited his unexpected guests and their captors to share his blessings.

Everyone enjoyed the big feast immensely and about four p.m. they again started on their way.

They rode all night, and half frozen, arrived at the Hays' ranch next morning, were fed and started off again. On December twenty-sixth at about two p.m. they arrived in Las Vegas, their captives in tow.

The Placita in Las Vegas was filled to overflowing with the curious who had been pouring into town all day, hoping to get a glimpse of the famous and infamous Billy the Kid. They came in from Sapello, Mora, Ocate, La Cueva, Rociada and all the surrounding villages and farms hoping to see the young bandit they had heard so much about.

On December twenty-eighth, 1880 *The Las Vegas Gazette* carried a good account of the proceedings, as well as an interview with the Kid which they had somehow wrangled out of Sheriff Romero. The lengthy article read:

INTERVIEW WITH BILLY BONNEY, THE BEST KNOWN MAN IN NEW MEXICO

With its accustomed enterprise *The Gazette* was the first paper to give the story of the capture of Billy Bonney (who has risen to notoriety under the sobriquet of "the Kid") Billy Wilson, Dave Rudabaugh, and Tom Pickett. Just at this time everything about the men is especially interesting, and after damning the party in general and "the Kid" in particular, through the columns of this paper, we consider it the correct thing to give them a show.

Through tthe kindness of Sheriff Romero, a representative of the Gazette was admitted to the jail yesterday morning. Mike Cosgrove, the obliging mail contractor, who has often met the boys while on business down the Pecos, had just gone in with four large bundles. The doors at the entrance stood open and a large crowd strained their necks to get a glimpse of the prisoners who stood in the passageway like children waiting for Christmas presents. One by one the bundles were unpacked, disclosing a good suit of clothes for each man. Mr. Cosgrove remarked that he wanted to see the boys go away in style.

Billy, the Kid and Billy Wilson who were shackled together stood up patiently while a blacksmith took off their shackles and bracelets to allow them an opportunity to make a change of clothing. Both prisoners watched the operation which was to set them free for a short while, but Wilson scarcely raised his eyes and spoke only once or twice to his compadre. Bonney, on the other hand, was light, chipper and very communicative, laughing, joking and chatting with bystanders.

"You appear to take it easy," the reporter said.

"Yes. What's the use of looking on the gloomy side of everything? The laugh's on me this time," he said. Then looking about the placita, Billy asked, "Is the jail at Santa Fe any better than this?"

This seemed to bother him considerably, for as he explained, "This is a terrible place to put a fellow in." He put the same question to everyone who came near him and when he learned that there was nothing better in store for him, he shrugged his shoulders and said something about putting up with what he had to.

He was the attraction of the show, and as he stood there, lightly kicking the toes of his boots on the stone pavement to keep his feet warm, one could scarcely doubt that he was the hero of the "Forty Thieves" romance which this paper had been running in serial form for six weeks or more.

"There was a big crowd gazing at me, wasn't there?" he exclaimed, and then smiling continued, "Well perhaps some of them will now think I'm half a man; everyone seemed to believe I was some kind of an animal." He did look human, indeed, but there was nothing very mannish about him in appearance; for he looked and acted a mere boy. He is about five feet eight or nine inches tall, lithe and slightly built, weighing about 140 pounds. He has a frank open countenance like a school boy with a trace of silky fuzz on his upper lip. His eyes are clear blue with a roguish snap about

This ominous-looking jail door is all that is left of the Las Vegas city jail where Billy and his cronies were incarcerated shortly after their capture at El ojo del Taiba on Dec. 23, 1880 "This is a terrible place to put a fellow in!"

them. His hair is light and his complexion fair. He is, in all, quite a handsome looking fellow, the only imperfection being two prominent front teeth which protruded like a squirrel's. In general, though he has agreeable and winning ways.

A cloud came over his face when he made some allusions to his being the hero of fabulous yarns, and something like indignation was expressed when he said that our extra issue misrepresented him in saying that he called his associates cowards. "I never said any such thing," he pouted. "I know they ain't cowards."

Billy Wilson was glum and sober, but from underneath his broad-brimmed hat, we saw a face that had by no means a bad look. He is light haired, with bluish-gray eyes, a little stouter than Bonney, and far quieter. He appeared ashamed and not in very good spirits. A final stroke of the hammer sent the final rivet on the bracelets, and they clanked on the pavement as they fell. Bonney straightened up and then rubbing his wrists where the sharp edged irons had chaffed him said: "I don't suppose you fellows would believe it but this is the first time I ever had bracelets on. But many an other better fellow has had them on too."

With Wilson he walked towards the little hole in the wall to the place which is no "sell" on a place of confinement. Just before entering he turned and looked back and exclaimed: "They say a fool for luck and a poor man for children. . .Garrett takes them all in."

We saw him again at the depot when the crowd presented a really warlike appearance. Standing by the car, out of one of the windows of which he was leaning, he talked freely with us of the whole affair.

"I don't blame you for writing of me as you have. You had to believe others stories; but then I don't know as anyone would believe anything good of me anyway." he said. "I wasn't the leader of any gang. I was for Billy all the time. About that Portales business, I owned the ranch with Charlie Bowdre. I took it up and was holding it because I knew that sometime a stage line would run

221

by there and I wanted to keep it for a station. But I found that there were certain men who would not let me live in the country and so I was going to leave. We had all our grub in the house when they took us in, and we were going to a place about six miles away in the morning to cook it and then light out. I haven't stolen any stock. I made my livingby gambling but that was the only way I could live. They wouldn't let me settle down; if they had I wouldn't be here today," and he held up the arm on which he had the bracelet. "Chisum got me into all this trouble and then wouldn't help me out. I went up to Lincoln to stand my trial on the warrant that was out for me, but the territory took a change of venue to Dona Aña and I knew that I had no show, and so I skinned out. When I went up to White Oaks the last time, I went there to consult with a lawyer, who had sent for me to come up. But I knew that I couldn't stay there either."

The conversation then drifted to the question of the final round-up of the party. Billy's story is the same as that given in our extra, issued at midnight on Sunday.

"If it hadn't been for the dead horse in the doorway I wouldn't be here. I would have ridden out on my bay mare and taken my chance of escaping," he said. "But I couldn't ride out over that, for she would have jumped back and I would have got it in the head. We could have stayed in the house but there wouldn't have been anything gained by that for they would have starved us out. I thought it was better to come out and get a square meal. . .don't you?"

The prospects of a fight exhiliarated him, and he bitterly bemoaned being chained. "If I only had my Winchester, I'd lick the whole crowd," was his confident comment on the strength of the attacking party. He sighed, and sighed again for a chance to take a hand in the fight and the burden of his desire was to be set free to fight on the side of his captors as soon as he could smell powder.

As the train rolled out, he lifted his hat and invited us

to call and see him in Santa Fe, calling out "Adios."

The Las Vegas Optic also had a series of articles on the capture. On December 28th, they wrote:

> The town was thrown into a fever of excitement by an announcement that the Kid and other members of his gang of outlaws had been captured and were nearing the city. The rumor was soon verified by the appearance in town of a squad of men led by Pat Garrett, deputy sheriff of Lincoln County, and Frank Stewart, of the Panhandle country, having in custody the Kid, Dave Rudabaugh, Billy Wilson and Tom Pickett. They were taken at once to the jail and locked up, and arrangements were made to guard the jail against any attempt to take the prisoners out and hang them. Feeling was particularly strong against Rudabaugh, who was an accessory to the murder of the Mexican jailer in an attempt to release Webb some months ago.

On the 31st the *Optic* also took a poke at the *Gazette* for "attempting to make a hero" out of Billy the Kid.

Getting out of Las Vegas was the problem now facing Sheriff Garrett. Sheriff Romero had attempted to keep Rudabaugh under confinement to face the warrant for Deputy Valdez's death and for escaping custody. Garrett knew if he succeeded, a necktie party would be the next thing on the agenda. He showed Romero his priority on the federal charges and finally the sheriff and the mob acquiesced, but not before the unruly mob had attempted to storm the train, only to be met by a gun at every door and window.

Pat mentioned that if it came to that, he'd put a gun in the hands of every one of his prisoners for his own defense. Billy's eyes brightened at the prospect; a good judge of character, he said, "All right, Pat, all I want is a six-shooter." Then looking at the crowd disgustedly, he added, "There is no danger, though; those fellows won't fight." He would have loved to get the painful shackles off and a hot six shooter in each fist. His rough, coarse fingers tightened on an imaginary stock as the train chugged off.

Six years after he had left La Villa Real de La Santa Fe at the tender age of fifteen, Billy was back. He had left the capitol city a bright-eyed teenager, his whole life ahead of him, and returned at the age of twenty-one with more accomplishments (if dubious) and with more adventures behind him than the average man experiences in a life time. That Billy had crammed a whole lifetime of excitements, adventures, troubles, and tribulations into such a short span would never be disputed. He had laid the foundations of a legend, unrivaled, and one that would live forever. He arrived at the Santa Fe train depot in Pat Garrett's custody on December 27, 1880 about 7:30 in the evening, where the group was met by U.S. Deputy Marshall Charley Conklin. Billy's first train ride had been fast and exciting, but it would also be his last.

After being wined and dined by the high and mighty in the capitol city for many days Pat Garrett, was finally able to tear himself away and return home to Lincoln where he received another hero's welcome. Billy, however, remained behind in a cold stone cell, chained to the floor.

On New Year's Day, he wrote a short note to Governor Lew Wallace, which said simply:

I would like to see you for a few moments if you can spare time.

Yours respectfully,
William H. Bonney

During one of her daily rounds of the jailhouse on March sixteenth, Sister Blandina Segale of Cincinnati, found him as she said, "with hands and feet cuffed and bound, and also chained to the floor." When the kindly Sister of Charity walked into his cell, Billy raised his head, and according to her in her daily diary, said: "I sure wish I could place a chair for you, Sister." His pluckiness and humor, even in adversity astounded the friendly sister considerably more than the sight of the heavy chains holding him to the floor.

On March 1, 1881, he attempted to escape but was soon discovered. He had tried to burrow through the cell's adobe and stone walls with whatever instruments he had been able to find, and was reported by another prisoner who wanted to curry favor with his keepers. Having failed in his escape attempt, he decided to try a different tack. On the second of March he dispatched another letter to Governor Lew Wallace.

Santa Fe, New Mexico
March 21, 1881

Governor Lew Wallace

Dear Sir:

I wish you would come down to the jail and see me. I have some letters which date back two years and there are parties who are very anxious to get them but I shall not dispose of them until I see you, that is, if you will come immediately.

Yours respectfully,
Wm. H. Bonney

Apparently, Billy had no trouble dispatching his communications, since two days later, as Milnor Rudulph's cousin James A. Garfield was being innaugurated, he sent him another, more desperate, more forceful letter, characteristically lacking in punctuation and capital letters.

Governor Lew Wallace

Dear Sir

I wrote you a little note the day before yesterday but
have received no answer I expect you have forgotten
what you promised me this month two years ago, but I
have not; and I think you had ought to have and seen
me as I requested you to. I have done everything that I
promised you I would and you have done nothing that
you promised me I think when you think the matter
over you will come down and see me as I can explain
everything to you.

Judge Leonard passed through here on his way east in
January and promised to come and see me on his way
back but he did not fulfill his "promise." it looks to me
like I am being left in the cold. I am not treated right by
Sherman. he lets every stranger that comes to see me
through curiosity in to see me, but will not let a single
one of my friends in, not even an attorney. I guess they
mean to send me up without giving me any show but
they will have a nice time doing it. I am not entirely
without friends I shall expect to see you some time
today.

Patiently waiting,
I am very truly yours,
W.H. Bonney

Twenty-three days later, after having almost lost all hope, he again fished for some response.

Governor Lew Wallace

Dear Sir

for the last time I ask. Will you keep your promise? I start below tomorrow. send answer by bearer.

Yours resp.
W. Bonney

The following day, March 28th, United States Deputy Marshall, Tony Neis took Bill Bonney and Billy Wilson from their cell. Dave Rudabaugh had already been transported back to Las Vegas to stand trail for killing of the deputy and escaping jail.

Delighted at being out of his shackles for the moment, Billy was a figure of gaiety and joy. When he learned that they would soon be leaving for Las Cruces and from there to La Mesilla, he joked with his jailers that he had never traveled so much or so well. As they climbed up into the comfortable Sulky, he looked back and waved, thanking his former jailors for a pleasant stay.

On April thirteenth, during the term of district court, Billy was tried for the murder of Buckshot Roberts three years before, and acquitted. The federal charges had been previously dismissed when the court realized that Blazer's Mill where Roberts had died was not on the Mescalero Apache Indian Reservation grounds, but was in fact right outside its boundaries and beyond their jurisdiction. Billy, then, was tried for the murder of Sheriff Brady at Lincoln by an all-Spanish jury, found guilty, and sentenced to hang. Unluckily, the date chosen for the hanging by the court was, Friday, the thirteenth day of May, 1881.

Chapter Fifteen

Death Comes to Famed Billy

Charlie Rudulph, now a spectator, more than a participant in the affair, added sixteen more stanzas to his saga of Billy the Kid, and entitled it "Muerte Del Afamado Bilito." My translation and interpretation follows:

Muerte del Afamado Bilito

1.

El bilecito mentado
Por penas bien merecidas,
Fue en Santa Fe encarcelado
Deudor de veinte y una vidas.
De Santa Fe a la mesilla
Requerido fue llevarlo,
El tubo mucha alegria
Viendo que era por pasearlo.

2.

La corte no tubo fallo
Pues fue su dever jusgar,
Y el dia trece de Mayo
Tenia que ser colgado.
Mas cambean las circumstancias
Y tambien las proposiciones,
Pues muchas fueron las ancias,
De los nobles corazones
Ejecutar la sentencia,
Que merecen los ladrones;
Pero sequire mi historia
Siendo que esta comenzada,
Pues es bastante notoria
Para no ser olvidada.

3.

De donde fue sentenciado
El Bill por justa razon,
A Lincoln fue transportado
Y encerrado en la prision,
A esperar el dia dado
Para hacer su ejecucion.
Bob Ollinger deputado
Y tambien Bell para ayuda
Fueron alli estacionados
Con estricta orden, sin duda,
De velar al sentenciado
Sin parcialidad ninguna.

4.

Siendo que toco quedar
Solo a Bell halle quidando,
Mientras Bob se fue a senar
Pues su ora seiba llegando
Y el Bill no estando dormido
Logro la oportunidad.
Y pronto se halla decedido,
De tomar su libertad.

5.

Pues las esposas tenia
En una mano las dos,
Y con toda su energia
Le dio un golpe tan feroz.
Que Bell cayo en sangre fria,
Sin aclamar a su dios.
Con la pistola de Bell
Con un balaso acabo,
De concluir su acto cruel,
Y luego se preparo.

6.

Bob cuando cenando estaba
Oyo un tiro resonar,
Sus pasos apresuraba
Sin acabar de cenar.
De la raya no paso
Donde tenia que quedar,
Halli el Bille lo mato.
Sin acabar de llegar.

Y asi el Bilito mentado
Anadio a su lista larga,
Dos, los pobres apreciados
Con su mano cruel y amarga,
Con winchester armado
Con pistola y municion,
Sale el Bilito malvado
Haciendo requisicion,
Que un caballo le ensillaran,
Con bastante precision.
Y haci en la caballeriza
Monto el caballo veloz,
Y con criminal sonriza,
Les dice a todos, "Adios."

A partes desconocidas
Se fue el Bilito mentado,
Y andando a las escondidas
Se ve ahora libertado.
Al oir del acto horroroso
Fue el grito del pueblo halzado,
Que Pat Garrett el famoso
Saliera en pos del malvado.
Con su determinacion
Tan firme y sin quebrantar,
Sale Pat con precision,
Sus amigos a vengar,

9.

Razon se habilla tenido
Que junto al bosque se hallava,
El bilecito escondido
Y que alli sin duda estaba.
Dos hombres Pat Garrett toma
de Lincoln cuando salio,
Sin tener ninguna broma
Al Fuerte se dirigio.

10.

Se oculta discretamente
Antes de entrar al lugar,
Cuando ya duerme la gente
Determina Pat entrar.
Con Pedro Maxwell fue a hablar
El Pat luego que llego,
Y al cuarto sin titubiar,
De Pedro se dirigio

11.

Pat con poco requisito
Da al Senor Maxwell su intento,
La causa de su visita
Aquella ora a su aposento.
No estarian un cuarto de ora
Ellos los dos platicando,
Cuando aquella inaudita hora
Ven un hombre al cuarto entrando.
Como que Pat al entrar
Dejo a sus dos compañeros
Parados en el portal,
Ellos ven al Bill primero.

12.

El Bill se acerca a la cama
Con bastante precaucion,
Pregunta a Pedro en voz sana
"Los de afuera, quienes son"?
Luego da trazas sacar,
Pat, su pistola al momento
Cuyo hizo al Bill recular
A causa del movimiento.

13.

El Bilito reculando,
Con su pistola asistada
A Pat sigue preguntando,
"Quien Es", pero no dispara.
Esto le dio a Pat lugar,
De poner su punto en giro
Y sin mas que demorar,
Le dejo ir un fatal tiro.
Al instante el Billy cayo,
Traspasado el corazon,
Y sin quejarse murio,
Cosa rara en un blazon.

14.

Es preciso mencionar,
Que el Bill en medias venia
Carne venia quitarle
A Don Pedro si tenia.
Cuando al cuarto el Bill entro,
El Pat estaba sentado,
De una ves lo conocio,
Se vio un poco asustado

15.

Con la muerte del Bilito,
Se halla este pueblo aliviado
Pues les dava temorcito,
Hallarse por el rodeado.
Por este acto tan afamado,
Que hizo a Pat tan importante
Merece ser bien premiado,
Por su accion tan arrogante.

16.

Ya concluyo el Bilecito
Despues de tan corta vida,
Cometio tanto delito,
Que su muerte fue aplaudida
Y haci siguio el Bilecito,
A sus compañeros buenos,
Tom Folliard y Charley Bawdrey
Pues no se podia menos.

MORAL

Juventud en general,
Los que lean esta historia
Fue el Bilito un ejemplar,
Con su vida tan notoria
Mas en que vino a quedar,
todo su gusto y su gloria
Pues no pudo a edad entrar,
Sin estar bajo custodia
Tenganlo en su memoria,
Lo que este jovan paso
De veinte un años murio,
Sin tener intrecesion
Y esto les suplico yo,
Tenganlo en su corazon.

FIN

—Charles M. Rudulph

Death Comes To Famed Billy

(an interpretive translation)

Since our historic capture of Billy the Kid on December 23, 1880, the territory had experienced an unprecedented peace and calm. The memorable incident had been hailed as a blessing by the vast majority of the body politic, but even those who still claimed friendship and advocacy to his cause, realized that what had happened at El Ojo del Taiba had truly been in their best interests. Many of the former bandits and killers were now either leaving the country one by one or attempting to settle down into peaceful pursuits. They knew that Garrett and his posse weren't fooling anymore.

Even though the posse that captured Billy may have had its share of unsavory characters the majority of them had been from honest, honorable families from the vicinity. It certainly did not compare unfavorably with the wild and woolly posses which had hunted him down on many previous occasions, such as the ones at the Jim Greathouse ranch and the McSween home.

There were more outlaws than lawmen after them at that time, and this was the main reason so many of the people, especially the Mexicans, had remained loyal to the Kid up to this day. The valid reasons for their loyalty cannot be denied since up to this time their poverty, and lack of education had been thoroughly exploited by the gringo, while Billy had always attempted to help and defend them.

They had seen him grow up among them in the last few years, from a clumsy unsure young prankster to a bold and daring gunslinger and leader. He had roamed the eastern and central plains of New Mexico until he knew every river, creek and waterhole, every mountain and even many an arroyo for a hundred miles around. Most importantly, he knew every farm and every ranch, every family, every brand and every steed. Always observant and shrewdly calculating, he carried in his wily mind a wealth of information necessary for his continued survival.

On April 21, 1881, Billy was taken to Fort Stanton, and from there to Lincoln by Deputy Sheriff Dave Woods and U.S. Deputy Marshall Robert Ollinger. He was jailed at the former Dolan-Murphy store which the county had just purchased for use as a jail; it was supposedly a very well fortified building. Nevertheless, Pat Garrett, with no intentions of losing his prize catch, deputized James W. Bell to help Ollinger guard him day and night. Since Billy had taken such an active part against them in the Lincoln County War, it was now charged that the old clique had exerted undue influence in the selection of the jurors for his trial, even intimidating them, and now influenced the circumstances of his incarceration.

Bell and Ollinger were issued the comfortable southeast apartment on the second floor, two doors down from the arsenal. Since there was no jail as such in the building yet, Billy would have to be guarded day and night in this room. The only entrance to the top floor was a wide outside stairway on the southwest side of the building. Bell had been a good friend of Jimmy Carlyle's who had been shot at the Greathouse ranch a few months before, but he did not appear to be holding a grudge against Billy for this killing.

We may perhaps assume that the two had reached some understanding in the matter, since Billy had never accepted responsibility for this one crime, claiming instead that Carlyle had been shot by his own men by mistake. Regardless of this, Billy's winning ways, his charming personality and friendliness soon won him over. With Ollinger it was different. He hated Billy with a passion and would often goad him into trying to escape, "so I can put a plug through his rotten hide," he said.

Bob Beckwith's death a few years before was the main reason for his hate and animosity; they had been good friends. In turn, Billy would charge him with having killed some of his friends, too.

On this fatal day, Bob Ollinger had taken some prisoners to supper across the street at the hotel, leaving James Bell in charge of the Kid. Bell and Billy played cards constantly to while the time away, as they were on this day. The friendly

239

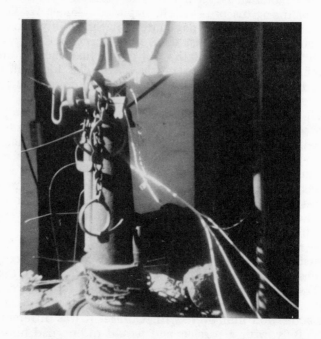

The handcuffs shown here are owned by the estate of Tom McGrath of Las Vegas. It is little wonder the Kid was able to fell James Bell with one ferocious blow—the handcuffs weigh about three pounds!

young guard had gotten rather lax in his duties and was becoming increasingly careless. On April 28, while Bob Ollinger was at the hotel, Billy decided to take advantage of his laxity. He also knew that he was not going to receive any help from Governor Wallace. He picked his handcuffs up from the table where they were playing cards, doubled them up in one hand, and catching him by surprise, gave Bell a savage blow to the side of the head. As he fell to the floor, Billy grabbed his gun and shot him in the back as the stunned man tried to escape down the stairs.

Bob Ollinger was still eating supper at the hotel when he heard the shot. He jumped up from the table and ran to the jail. When he reached the building, he looked up to the balcony; standing there with a diabolical grin on his face, was Billy, Ollinger's shotgun in his hands. "Hello, Bob," he said as he pulled the trigger. Ollinger's brains splattered all over the hard packed road.

Billy looked down disdainfully, his eyes mere slits on his face. He went back into the building, picked up a Winchester, two six-shooters and ammunition and raced to the corral. Once there, he ordered Godfrey Gaus, cook and stable hand, to saddle up a horse for him quick, and grabbed a blanket as he raced from the scene.

Many people from the village went out to see him and to wish him well. He shook hands all around, mounted his horse, looked back and waved and bade them all adios. "Adios, Bilito, con mucho cuidado. Vaya con Dios—Que te vaya bien, Billy," the villagers chorused.

For many years, the closest witness, Godfrey Gaus, had absolutely refused to discuss the escape until finally in 1890, he agreed to an interview with *The Lincoln County Leader*, and broke his silence. Recounting his recollections, he confessed one tidbit of information; he had "thrown a little prospecting pick" to Billy through the window. Parts of his lengthy article follow:

> Once upon a time it was, if I mistake not, in the middle of the month of April, 1880, 1881, or perhaps 1882, while Sam Wortley and myself were raising a

vegetable garden behind the courthouse at Lincoln, that
Billy the Kid was brought back from Dona Ana County
where he was tried for murder and sentenced to be
hanged in Lincoln. About a week after that date he
killed his two keepers and escaped. As the county had
no jail then, he was kept under guard in the upper story
of the courthouse. Sam and myself lived in a house
together behind the courthouse. That memorable day I
came out of my room whence I had gone to light my
pipe, and was crossing the yard behind the courthouse.
Somebody was hurrying downstairs and Deputy Sheriff
Bell was emerging from the door, running towards me.
He ran right into my arms, expiring the same moment,
and I laid him down dead. That I was in a hurry to
secure assistance or perhaps to save myself everyone will
believe.

When I arrived at the garden gate leading to the street
in front of the courthouse, I saw the other deputy
sheriff, Ollinger, coming out of the hotel opposite with
the other four or five county prisoners where they had
taken their dinner. I called to him to come quick. He
did so, leaving his prisoners in front of the hotel. When
he had come close up to me, and while standing not
more than a yard apart, I told him that I was just after
laying Bell dead on the ground in the yard behind.
Before he could reply he was struck by a well-directed
shot fired from a window above us, and fell dead at my
feet. I ran for my life to reach my room and safety
when Billy the Kid called to me.

"Don't run, I wouldn't hurt you—I am alone and
master not only of the courthouse but also of the town,
for I will allow nobody to come near us. You go," he
said, "and saddle one of Judge Leonard's horses and I
will clear out as soon as I can have the shackles loosened
from my legs."

With a little prospecting pick I had thrown to him
through the window, he was working for at least an
hour and could not accomplish more than to free one
leg. He came to the conclusion to await a better chance,

tie one shackle to his waist-belt and start out. Meanwhile I had saddled a small skittish pony belonging to Billy Burt as there was no other horse available and had also, by Billy's command, tied a pair of red blankets behind the saddle. I came near forgetting to say that whilst I was busy saddling and Mr. Billy Kid trying hard to get his shackles off, my partner Sam Wortley appeared in the door leading from the garden where he had been at work into the yard and that when he saw the two sheriffs lying there dead he did not know whether to go in or retreat, but on Billy the Kid's assurance that he would not hurt him he went in and made himself generally useful. When Billy went downstairs at last, on passing the body of Bell he said, "I am sorry I had to kill him, but I couldn't help it." On passing the body of Ollinger he gave him a tap with his boot saying, "You are not going to round me up again." We went out together where I had tied up the pony, and he told me to tell the owner of same, Billy Burt, that he would send it back next day. I, myself, didn't much believe in his promise, but, sure enough next morning the pony arrived safe and sound at the courthouse in Lincoln, trailing a long lariat. And so Billy the Kid started out that evening, after he had shaken hands with everybody around and after having had a little difficulty in mounting on account of the shackles on his leg, rejoicing on his way.

From Lincoln he rode west towards Fort Stanton, then north through Baca Canyon towards the ranch of his friend Juan Padilla where he left the horse and took off on foot up the canyon to Jose Cordova's house a few miles west of Padilla's.

Happy to see him, Cordova and his son Manuel helped him to remove the heavy shackles. They had rubbed his skin raw and it had started to bleed. Cordova wanted him to rest up and stay overnight so that he could minister to his wounds. "Se van a enconar," he said, but Billy reneged; he had to get to Ygenio's as soon as possible; besides, the posse was probably not too far behind.

Late that night, nearing exhaustion, Billy staggered into his good friend Ygenio Salazar's place in Las Tablas at the base of the Capitanas, where he received an exuberant welcome from Ygenio and his wife. After a good hot supper, Salazar tried his best to convince Billy to leave the territory for good, to go to Mexico, or Arizona and start a new life. "Te van a matar," he said, deeply concerned.

"No se preocupe, compadre," Billy said, "You know I can take care of myself."

Early next morning, Billy left for Fort Sumner; he had to see Celsa before he left. The trek across the desert from Las Tablas is about ninety miles as the crow flies, so without really knowing we may assume that he either borrowed another horse from Salazar or he was the rogue who stole one from Andy Richardson's corral that night. He escaped on the twenty-eighth of April, and nothing was known of him until sometime in June when little rumors started cropping up that he had been seen here or there around Fort Sumner, Mesilla or Las Cruces, or at the cow and sheep camps by the Arenoso.

The newspapers had been in an uproar over the escape and the killing of Bell and Ollinger, and their daily headlines continued to push the much hated "Santa Fe Ring" line. The man they were trying to pass off as the great protector of the people, the efficient officer, "cut down in the prime of ripe manhood," Bob Ollinger, was already well known by the people. It was he they remembered, whose grudge against Juan Chavez of Seven Rivers must have been so strong that when they met in the street one day and Chavez extended his hand Ollinger clasped it with his left and with his right shot him right in the bowels at close range. Chavez had left a big family!

When he helped arrest Bob Jones for a misdemeanor, he made it appear that Jones had attempted to escape, and shot him three times, all in the back. He killed John Hill under the same treacherous circumstances. Pat Garrett often told a tale about when Ollinger and he had gone to arrest a Mexican, also for a minor offense, and they had found him hiding in a ditch behind his house. Pat placed him under arrest and was leading him to his horses when Ollinger, with the most "devilish expression I've ever seen," (Pat's words) came running up, his gun ready in his hand. "Let me kill 'im, Pat, let me kill 'im," he insisted mercilessly.

Afterwards, Pat said, "Ollinger was a born murderer. He was the only man I ever knew whom I believe was literally bloodthirsty."

Susan Barber, McSween's widow, also said once, "After Ollinger was killed, I met his mother. Out of courtesy, I expressed my sympathy to her in what I supposed was her bereavement. I was greatly shocked when the old woman said to me, "Bob was a murderer from his cradle, and if there is a hell, I know he is there." Maybe that is the reason that no one came to his aid, or attempted to stop Billy; maybe that is why everyone shook his hand and waved as he rode leisurely away.

Incensed over the inaction of the people of Lincoln, *The Las Vegas Optic* wrote on May 3rd: "After killing Bell and Ollinger the Kid compelled Mr. Goss to saddle Mr. William Burt's horse for him, and rode quietly and leisurely out of town, no one offering to molest him in any way. The pusillanimity of such conduct by a whole town and that town the county seat, is almost incredible. Yet such is the fact."

Throughout the month of June, nothing was heard about Billy. He was doing a good job evading his would-be captors, and even though rumors persisted, few people knew of his whereabouts.

On the second of July, 1881, the Rudulph household was thrown into a dither together with the rest of the country President Garfield had been shot. For days all the information they had was that he had been slain by an assassin by the name of Charles Guiteau; soon however, they found out that he had not died instantly and in fact lingered between life and death for two and a half months more.

Saddened by the cruel fate which had befallen his beloved cousin Lucretia, Milnor Rudulph sent her a communication to Washington. On July 13, 1881, Maria Candelaria Trujillo y

Rudulph glanced out of her kitchen window at Sunnyside to see a strange man approaching the house.

Quien sera? she thought. Han venido tantos trampes. The influx of foreigners into New Mexico and the southwest had brought them nothing but trouble. Puras desgracias.

"Milnor," she called to her husband, "hay viene un hombre a caballo." I hope it's not about the president, she thought.

"Oh, no," thought Milnor, "el Bilito," and then, "No, no es," out loud as he peered out, unlatching the heavy bolt on the door.

"Good morning," Rudulph said as he greeted the heavyset well-built young man; "what can I do for you?"

Sheriff Garrett has sent me to see you, sir," answered the stranger. "May I come in?"

"Of course, Rudulph said. "Please do, please come in."

"I'm John Poe," the man introduced himself, alighting from his horse, "and I represent the Canadian River Cattle Growers Association from Fort Elliott, Texas. We've come up here to see if we can do something to help Garrett round up Billy the Kid and his bandits, and he thinks you might be able to help. Garrett sent you this," he continued, handing Rudulph a note.

"No," Rudulph said, after reading the note, "we haven't seen him for quite a while. I think it was late in the fall when he stopped by last, and we haven't seen him since. . .Billy," he added for Maria Candelaria's benefit. She nodded in agreement.

"We've heard lots of rumors," Rudulph continued, "that he's right here in Sumner, but frankly, I believe he's got a bit more sense than that. I believe he's out somewhere in Arizona, probably in Tombstone where he's got friends. That Johnny Ringo used to be a good friend of his. Wouldn't surprise me if they haven't already teamed up together, unless Wyatt Earp, the marshall, got Ringo by now. . . haven't heard. . . ." His words trailed off.

Maria Candelaria thought wistfully, sadly, back to that day when she'd told Billy to keep away from the baby's milk—she should have let him drink some—he was such a nice boy, really. She'd wept at night and prayed for him, thinking that he might be out in the cold somewhere. She remembered the meal she'd made, fit for company, and he had eaten as if he hadn't had a bite to eat for a week. "No," she suddenly thought, "that must have been the time before, because the last time I didn't even invite him into the house on Milnor's orders. Pobrecito. It must have been the time before."

He had told them another of his scary tales of *brujas* that night, she remembered with a chuckle; the one about Doña Peipeiuta, the mean old witch from Le Fèbre, who with a twist of the wrist and some strange devilish incantations could take every part of her body apart. His friend's father's great-uncle had seen it firsthand, he had declared, adding a ring of authenticity to his harrowing tale. The brave man had peeked into her window one moonlit night when he was a young man. There was a full moon out and coyotes were howling and cats were screeching when he tiptoed to her window. He wanted to find out if what he had heard about her was true.

It took his eyes a while to adjust to the dimly lit kitchen, black candles flickering eerily here and there. Finally, his eyes grew accustomed to the gloom, and sure enough there was Doña Peipeiuta perched on the handmade wooden bench which poor old Don Ruperto had made for her. He had died a horrible death for his kindness, they said, screaming painfully until the end. . .*embrujado*. His insides had turned to stone.

Doña Peipeiuta was sitting there smugly in the middle of her kitchen, bathing herself in her old wooden tub, fiendishly cackling to herself all the while. First she pulled off a leg at the knee, scrubbed it well in the bloody water, then put it back on with a practised twist. She then pulled off an ear, an arm, and so on; then with a blood-curdling screech, she tore off her head, submersing it in the water until it bubbled, and began to scrub its hair. She held it firmly between her legs as she scrubbed it, while its yellow bug eyes stared blankly at the bloody stump.

Most of his skin had crawled up his collar by this time and his hair was standing up straight. He was having a hard time containing himself because he just knew that he was going to haul off through the weeds any time now, screaming bloody murder, when she finally started to dress.

She picked her dirtiest, most used, most wrinkled, long, drab black dress, cobwebs at the creases, grabbed a dusty, ragged black *tapalo* from behind the door, dislodging some black widows; took her trusty old broom, patted her horned black cat, and snapping her crooked, bony fingers, said a few more strange sounding incantations and disappeared into the night with a bang, leaving behind a smelly black cloud.

Only then did he get his long skinny legs into action, but he wasn't getting anywhere—his fingers wouldn't let go of the fence. Finally he was able to pry them loose, and with eyes big as lanterns lighting his way, his hair magnetized like porcupine quills, he tore off through the night, knocking over the outside privy. It was lucky for him that she had been in such a big hurry to be first at the witches' Saturday night dance, or she would surely have taken off after him. Of course one thing to his advantage, and the only reason he didn't go loco, was that he was a "Juan"; everyone knows that if a Juan makes the sign of the cross and draws a ring around himself "there ain't no witch that'll even get close to him," Billy concluded.

"Isn't," Emilia had corrected.

John Poe was leaving, snapping her out of her goose-pimpled reverie. Garrett was waiting for him just outside of town, Poe said as he left.

Maria Candelaria shivered, and went back to her cleaning chores.

"Where were you?" Rudulph asked; "you didn't hear a word we said." "How embarrassing," she replied, "I must have been daydreaming." She had taken down the *manta* covering the rafters, washed it and had been tacking it back up when the stranger arrived. In a confused silence she tugged at the huge cloth on the floor, stretching it into shape. She'd wanted the house to be as clean as possible while she was gone.

After what seemed like years of planning, she was finally

leaving Monday for Las Vegas and Rociada for an extended visit, and maybe to pave the way for the family's return to the beloved green mountains of her youth. Besides, she wanted to see her father who was already sixty-seven years old, and her mother who was also getting on in age. She hadn't seen them for a long time. Tillie, Milnor, Emilia and cousin Jenny, who lived with them now since her mother's death, would be going along too, while Charles Frederick would be staying with his father at the ranch.

The loneliness of the long days and nights without his wife and family were attested to by Milnor Rudulph when he wrote and sent the following impassioned poem to his wife.

To My Wife On Her Prolonged Absence

You are far away from home, and I'm wondering, my love,
How you have been passing the day;
And I'm sending prayers to our maker above,
For you and my bairn's far away.

My Jennie so brave and so loving,
My golden-haired Tillie, so bright,
And where in the world is my Minnie, now roaring?
Alone, with his sheep this dark night.

It is long since you left and long till you come,
Darling, how can you delay?
Have you no heartstrings pulling you home?
Or say, does it please you to stay?

Bethink you how long I've been praying,
And longing to see my sick child.
Oh, hasten your coming; why are you staying?
This torture will sure drive me wild.

Mr. Milnor Rudulph
Sunnyside, New Mexico
July 28, 1881, 11:00 P.M.

Even though Rudulph had been unable to offer John Poe any concrete information as to Billy's whereabouts, they still concentrated their efforts in the Fort Sumner area.

Pat Garrett had heard that Billy was hiding out in nearby El Bosque, the same woody area from which they had ridden into Fort Sumner that fateful night last December when Tom Folliard had died. So he had ridden quietly into the sleeping village with deputies Poe and McKinney.

The trio waited patiently in the *placita* until the lights went out in most of the houses, and then quietly they made their way across it. Billy would check first with Don Pedro Maxwell, Pat figured, as they made their way through the dense peach orchard north of the house, then alongside the old adobe wall which surrounded the property. When they were parallel to the porch they easily scaled the wall at the deeply eroded crevice, which had been made by countless feet before them; they used it as a shortcut.

Pat then entered the west side of the porch cautiously, whispering to his deputies to keep quiet and wait outside. He then tiptoed across the porch and into Don Pedro's house, leaving the two deputies outside in the shadows of the house. The bedroom door was unlocked, so Garrett, obviously knowing his way around, went in and sat on the bed, startling the sleeping man.

After he calmed down, they talked quietly in the dark for a few minutes. . .it was a quarter to twelve.

About eight minutes before midnight, Billy stole soundlessly through the warm summer night, a sharp knife in his hand. He intended to carve himself a piece of meat from a beef hanging in Don Pedro Maxwell's porch, high up away from the dogs. He had left his boots by the cot in the little room he was sharing with a Mexican friend next to the Gutierrez house, and now as he quietly crossed the porch in his socks, he perceived a movement in the dark. Two figures were standing flat against the house. Pat's deputies too had been caught by surprise.

Swiftly, Billy jumped inside, barging into Maxwell's dark bedroom, asking in Spanish, "Los de afuera, quienes son?" (Those outside, who are they) "Quienes son, Pedro?" he repeated.

Recognizing him, Pat went for his gun, and Billy, catching the gesture in the dark through the corner of his eye, spun around, gun in hand and again asked Maxwell, "Quien es; quien es?" He kept on repeating the question, giving Pat half a second's advantage, just barely enough time to shoot first.

Billy fell mortally wounded by the stove, the bullet finding its mark in his left breast in the area right above the heart. He died instantly, without making a sound, following the footsteps of his two old companions Tom Folliard and Charley Bowdre.

It was said that Don Pedro Maxwell, scared completely out of his wits, streaked past Pat Garrett over Billy's dead body and out the door, trailing a cortege of blankets and bed clothes behind, screaming in bloody terror, "Don't shoot me, don't shoot me!" Thereafter among his jesting friends, he was to be known instead of as Don Pedro, by the nickname of "Don Chootme."

Pat Garrett, overjoyed by his accomplishment, ran out on the porch, jumping up and down with excitement, screaming, "Mate al Chivito, mate al Chivito." (I've killed the kid, I've killed the kid.) "Whoopee, mate al Chivito."

With the loud gun blast and Pat's childish glee, the whole household was instantly awake and in an uproar. Upon hearing the commotion, Deluvina Maxwell ran from her room in her nightgown, barging past Pat Garrett and pushing him aside as he jumped for joy, running into the room now lit by a dim oil lamp. On the floor by the stove was Billy, his shirt pulled open to show a bullet hole in his chest. A painful wail tore from the depths of her soul as the dark brown woman fell on her knees beside him and cradled his head in her arms, tears streaming down her face.

"Pobrecito mi Bilito, mi muchachito," she cried in anguish, then catching sight of Garrett who was still strutting around like a rooster and patting himself on the back, she screamed, "Desgraciado, Tejano cabron," shaking her fists at him. Words she had never before used came easily to her bereaved mind. "Matates a mi Bilito, asessino desgraciado." He was her *chivito*, her *hijito*; she had taken care of him. She had never had a son of her own and Billy had been so alone.

Celsa broke into the scene, also sobbing, her fists pounding on Garrett's chest, his face, calling down on his head every Spanish curse she could think of.

Nasaria, Abrana, Paulita Maxwell, Dona Luz and many others gathered together, faces pale, weeping, talking softly, consoling each other. In the background, hammering was heard from the carpentry shop where Don Jose and his nephew worked feverishly in the dim light on a rough white pine box, each hammer blow sadly tolling out the bad news until the church bells took over the sad lament.

Outside, clusters of angry, heavily armed young Mexican men shook their fists at the deputies and Garrett, cursing them all, while others shook his hand and patted him on the back. Opposing feelings and opinions over the death ran rampant throughout the village and the territory as the news spread in a matter of hours, this schism would exist for months and even years to come.

Upon hearing the news, Milnor Rudulph called Charley from his bed, and together they sped through the night to Fort Sumner, where upon arrival they found nothing but confusion, anger and dissention. Some wanted to hang Garrett and his deputies, who had found it wise to retreat and were now secluded in a room in Maxwell's house, their guns in hand. Others wanted them rewarded.

Alejandro Segura, the justice of the peace, had been happy to see his friend Rudulph, whom he knew was of unquestionable integrity and clear-thinking. He appointed him to head the coroner's jury, and together they picked other prominent level-headed leaders of the community to fill the remaining five seats.

They met over the Kid's body and with no argument or dissent unanimously agreed on the following report given below translated from its original Spanish.

Territory of New Mexico
San Miquel County
Precinct Twenty-Seven
First Judicial District

Greetings to the Attorney General,
Territory of New Mexico.

This fifteenth day of July, 1881, the undersigned justice of the peace received information that there had been a death in Fort Sumner in said precinct and immediately upon receiving the information proceeded to the said place and named Milnor Rudulph, Jose Silva, Antonio Saavedra, Pedro Antonio Lucero, Lorenzo Jaramillo, and Sabal Gutierrez a jury to investigate the matter.

The said jury convening in the house of Luz B. Maxwell proceeded to a room in said house where they found the body of William Bonney, alias "the Kid" with a bullet wound in his breast on the left side of the chest.

The jury has arrived at the following dictamen:

We of the jury unanimously find that William Bonney has been killed by a bullet entering the left side of his chest in the region of the heart, and shot from a gun in the hands of Pat F. Garrett, and our dictum is that the act of said Garrett was justifiable homicide and we are of the opinion that the gratitude of the whole community is owed to said Garrett for his deed, and that he deserves to be rewarded.

It was signed by M. Rudulph, president, Antonio Saavedra, Pedro Antonio Lucero, Jose Silba, Sabal Gutierrez and Lorenzo Jaramillo.

Then below the signatures it reads: Information all of which I place at your disposal, Alejandro Segura, Justice of the Peace

Thus, with a brief and impersonal two-hundred-word report, the six honorable men affixed their signatures and marks to the post mortem on William Bonney, "Billy the

Kid," valorous, enigmatic, twenty-one-year-old bandit of the west.

Only his spirit remained, to soar freely over his beloved land, cause of his death. It would peek down longingly at Las Cañaditas, where he had often found peace among the *Piñones*; at Las Verandas, where he had rested confidently many a time; at Los Portales where he had dreams of settling down on a little ranch, and it would look down on the little bench under the old apple tree in the church yard in Fort Sumner, where he had had long serious discussions with the padre and had just begun to understand himself.

It would look down on his beloved, fitfully trying to sleep, and pause momentarily to gaze lovingly on her face one last time. He has passed on into eternity to meet his God, to face his dreaded judgment, twenty-one accusing fingers, leaving behind a legend. No more does he roam the valleys, but he does not bemoan his fate; for Billy was prepared; he knew the law by which he lived, he knew his day of reckoning would come. As Deluvina Maxwell said, "That boy rests in peace."

La Golondrina Taosena

Oh, cuanto envidio al mirar que te alejas
    Ave feliz, de dicha y de placer,
Mis ayes lleva a la laguna negra
    Que nunca, nunca, nunca olvidare.
Y cuando llegues, a mis hijos abrasa,
    Y a mis hermanos y sobrinos tambien.
Y tiernamente les daras mi embajda,
    Y cuanto siento no poder ir tambien.

Del Rio Grande hasta la laguna,
    Se extiende el echo de mi triste voz,
Y lloro y pido, pido con ternura,
    El bienestar de mis hijos los dos,
Y a mis hermanos y sobrinos queridos
    Dios los bendiga, por su santo amor,
Y ellos haci a mis hijos inspiren
    El santo amor y temor a Dios.

Tillie R. Trambley
Dec. 20, 1905